RVers' Guide to
SOLAR BATTERY CHARGING

12 volt DC–120 volt AC Inverters

by Noel and Barbara Kirkby

Updated edition 1993

aatec publications
PO Box 7119, Ann Arbor, Michigan 48107
313/995 1470 phone & fax

Library of Congress Cataloging-in-Publication Data
Kirkby, Noel.
    RVers' guide to solar battery charging. 12 volt DC-120 volt AC.
    Includes index.
    1. Recreational vehicles—Batteries. 2. Solar batteries.
I. Kirkby, Barbara.
II. Title.
TL298.K57   1987 629.2'542 87-19611
ISBN 0-937948-08-X

Manufactured in the United States of America

Cover Design by Carl Benkert

Noel and Barbara Kirkby live in a solar home in the desert foothills near Phoenix, Arizona. They travel each summer in an RV and found that the traditional methods of battery charging did not meet their needs. The search for a better method began and resulted in the purchase of a solar electric system. Their present RV is completely independent electrically. It is an example to those seeking peace and freedom from engine generators and crowded campgrounds.

Noel and Barbara's experiences and their efforts in researching and designing their own system led to the creation of their business—RV Solar Electric—which designs, tests, and constantly improves solar equipment for the RV. They now manufacture, package, and distribute the RV POWERPAC™ and BATTERY GUARD™, and publish a semi-annual newsletter, *Solar Electric Update,* to share the new information and helpful hints generated by the many solar and soon-to-be-solar RVers throughout the country.

This book is dedicated to our beloved parents
Samuel and Ruth Kirkby
and
Glenn and Jewell Warren
whose love for the great outdoors introduced us
to the RV lifestyle during its infancy

And to our three children
Doug, Kim, and Steve
who have shared many an RV adventure with us
and who, in turn, will be
passing on this love to the next generation.

Contents

OUR SOLAR EXPERIENCES

by Barbara Kirkby

Noel and I have been serious RVers since 1966, and trips of extended length have been an important part of our family life. We started with a 12-foot trailer and, as our three children grew, we graduated through a succession of larger trailers to our present class A motorhome.

In 1977 we learned all about dry camping, or "boon-docking," when we spent six months at the base of the Sierras beside a delightful trout stream. Our greatest concern was battery power for the water pump, lights, and heater, and we found that even strict conservation practices were not enough to maintain an adequate power supply.

We used three batteries in rotation with the tow vehicle battery and had to drive endless miles just to get a half-way charge. Buying a generator only created more headaches in the form of annoying adjustments, repairs, noise, and fuel handling. When the snow arrived, we could not keep up with the demands of the furnace blower and acquired a catalytic heater that proved to be a big help in keeping our electric consumption down. But, there still had to be a better way to charge those cold batteries.

Solar was the answer! Our first solar charging system, in 1979, introduced us to a concept of RV independence that still amazes me. Two solar panels flat atop the roof quietly generated enough power to meet the basic energy needs of our family of five. Since that time, remarkable breakthroughs, especially in high-efficiency inverters, have added even more exciting dimensions to our RV adventures. With our inverter we now have 120-volt utility-like current at will—even when camped independent of electrical hook-ups for an entire summer. By simply adding two solar panels and deep-cycle batteries, a total of four each, we can *produce* and *store* a surplus reserve of power.

We easily meet our 12-volt needs and have plenty of power left to run the inverter, which in turn supplies 120-volt current for our microwave, vacuum, blender, hair dryer, sewing machine, and even power tools. Our POWER GUARD regulator/meter set-up is an indispensable aid for monitoring our private "power company." It tells us how much we are storing and how much we are charging at any given time, and so helps us gauge how extravagant we can be or how conservative we must be in our power consumption.

Recently, our motorhome broke down in the most desolate part of Death Valley. What a place to discover that the alternator and bracket had broken away from the engine, leaving the bolts sheared off in the engine block! Our solar panels generated the electricity that allowed us to remove the broken alternator and continue on the road to home for convenient, and inexpensive, repairs.

When Noel was first searching for a photovoltaics source, I recall that my attitude was skeptical at best. To hear him explain it, some magical piece of glass would soak up the sun's energy and abracadabra . . . all the power our RV would need. Well, since 1979 we have been using these "magical, silent, maintenance-free generators" in our RV and for supplemental power in our home. Now I not only enjoy all the comforts of our solar-powered RV, but, with Noel and our three teenagers, understand and enthusiastically endorse the benefits of this simple technology.

We wrote this book for the RVer who seeks the independence and comfort we have found. Even though it contains lots of technical detail, the basics are included, too. We remember what it was like when we hardly knew a watt from an amp, and no one could answer all our questions. You'd be surprised at the number of people on the road who ask us how much hot water our panels produce. A little reading and research will clear up many misconceptions about what solar power can do—and how much it will cost.

We have tried to include all the information you will need to investigate, decide, size, select, purchase, and install solar components or packaged systems in your RV. If you have difficulties or questions, just write or phone us. We're always glad to hear from other RVers—to offer technical assistance and share the benefits of solar battery charging. We hope you enjoy the book!

1
INTRODUCTION

RV owners are several steps ahead of conventional homeowners when it comes to going solar. RVs come with a ready-made, low-voltage power system. You just have to choose among the battery charging options—which include solar—to power it. They are, by necessity, designed for efficiency—a major consideration when producing your own power. Large RVs are very much like small cabins: The limited space provides the opportunity for saving energy and dollars. As for the assumption that RVs are frivolous fuel-wasters, a retired RVer seldom travels more than 6000 miles per year. The working homeowner travels well over 10,000 miles annually just getting to work and running errands.

A 30-foot RV, properly insulated, can be heated comfortably with only three ounces of propane per hour. Because of limited storage, water conservation becomes routine. With a low water-usage toilet, a couple requires only about 30 gallons per week total—less than the amount used *daily* in the average home for toilet flushing. And when you can't find the space or supply the energy for that 20 cubic foot frostless fridge, you realize you don't need it anyway—nor many of the gimmicky appliances that line the kitchen shelves at home.

With the low-energy needs of an RV, we can live quite comfortably on a moderate amount of electricity. And, we can produce the electricity ourselves at a reasonable price. Careful planning is required. Conservation is the key.

Photovoltaics (PV), the technology of converting sunlight into electricity via solar cells, came to the attention of the general public during the early days of the space program. Today, solar cells and solar panels power everything from toys, calculators, wristwatches, and radios to water pumps, airplanes, and homes. In contrast to fossil fuel generators and utility power—complicated, costly, and high-maintenance technologies—PV simply produces power quietly, safely, and with minimal maintenance. Long considered too expensive for practical applications, solar electricity today is a cost-efficient and attractive alternative, especially when utility hook-ups are not available or not desired.

Solar electricity is ideally suited to RV use for a number of reasons.

- Reliability: High-quality solar systems are available today
- Long life: Design life of 20 to 30 years; carries 10-year manufacturer's warranty
- Portability and ease of installation
- "Gentle" charging process that prolongs battery life substantially
- Minimal maintenance required
- No moving parts—and so no replacement of worn-out components
- No handling of messy fuels or equipment
- Philosophical compatibility with the concept of RVing
- No noxious fumes, no pollution, no noise
- Cost-efficient in comparison with other RV systems—no cost after initial investment and actually less expensive when amortized over just a few years
- Fuel is free—sunlight!

Another important feature of a solar battery charging system is its modular construction. You may start small, to fit within your budget, and expand your system as needs or desires dictate. We recommend, as a matter of fact, that you start with a modest solar system of one or two panels, learn to use energy efficiently, and add on as you gain experience.

Solar electricity is a technology that makes sense. It is our objective to describe a "total energy system" concept of battery charging—that is, how to combine *all* the available RV power sources into an independent, effective "power company" which *you* control.

This is the book for you if you—
1. want detailed information on RV electrical systems, how they work, and how to make them less costly and more reliable.
2. use RV park hook-ups or generators, but because of their limitations and increasing costs want an independent power source as an option.
3. desire complete energy independence and the freedom it affords—the freedom to choose location and length of stay, without a noisy, troublesome generator and away from crowded campgrounds.

Chapter 2 begins with a basic discussion of electricity and defines the terms that will be used throughout the book. Don't worry. It's all in layman's terms, and there are no complicated mathematics. We will also describe the concepts behind solar electricity and the output characteristics of solar panels—in just enough detail. There's a good reason for this. Many people just can't believe how simple the whole business really is and sometimes complicate it unnecessarily. For those of you who do want more information on the technological parameters and the actual manufacture of solar cells, we have included an overview in Appendix A.

In chapter 3 we go into great detail on the subject of batteries because we have found that an enormous amount of misinformation exists on their selection, use, and care. Proper selection and charging techniques, simple but regular maintenance, and periodic analysis and testing will result in greatly extended battery life.

Our discussion also addresses the functions of conventional RV power sources—the alternator, the generator, and the power converter.

Our own experiences and those of many other RVers have resulted in a large file of how-to tips about living with low-voltage electricity. Chapter 4 stresses the importance of conservation and how to achieve it as it pertains to lighting, entertainment systems, appliances and DC conversions, water systems, heating, cooling, and refrigeration in the RV.

Although we introduce solar concepts, facts, and tips throughout, chapter 5 is devoted entirely to the solar battery charging option—its components, system regulation, and costs. Sizing a solar system—how many panels, how much battery capacity—can be difficult. We've included a "Custom Design Worksheet" and actual detailed examples submitted by RVers you might know to help you design the system that's best for you.

Chapter 6 describes the dual 12-volt DC/120-volt AC wiring system in the RV. Understanding this is essential to the safe, efficient installation of your solar battery charging system. Then, we provide illustrated, step-by-step instructions for actual solar system installation and how to tie-in to your existing wiring set-up.

Many RVers are now experiencing the convenience of on-board 120-volt AC with a high-efficiency inverter. Chapter 7 addresses the types of inverters now available, the increased power options afforded by their use, and their compatibility with an RV solar system.

We do mention products, some of our own manufacture and those of others. If we recommend something, it has proven reliable through our own use and testing. Our resource appendix, Appendix B, includes listings for manufacturers and suppliers of the products and publications cited in the book.

Before you go on, scan the questions listed below. Maybe one is yours. We have received countless inquiries over the years, indicating the interest people have in RV battery charging alternatives. And that's the reason for this book. We hope it gives you the information you need to join the increasing ranks of RVers who have chosen the solar alternative.

QUESTIONS & ANSWERS

How can I determine if solar will work for me?

Study, read, and ask questions. This book is a good beginning. You must determine your RV lifestyle and expectations, then match them to a system.

Will solar take care of all my RV energy needs?

That's up to you. To answer this question, you must determine the amount of electricity your appliances consume. A small motor-home or trailer with few lights and a TV can be totally served by one solar panel. Larger units, more people, longer stays require more panels.

Does a solar panel require maintenance?

Hardly ever. Solar panels are impervious to almost all weather conditions, but if hail is breaking automotive windshields, it might break the glass on the solar panel. Keep your comprehensive insurance in force. An occasional cleaning when dusty conditions prevail will aid output. Tilt panels to face south in winter to increase power generated. Keep them flat in the other seasons. Panels are basically self-maintaining.

Is it easy to convert my RV to solar power?

Easier than you think. Because an RV already has a 12-volt DC system, you only need to position the solar panels and connect the positive and negative wires to the RV battery.

What is the life expectancy of a solar panel?

In the photovoltaic process, there is nothing to "use up." Technically, then, a a solar panel—unless broken—has an unlimited lifetime.

Is a solar system expensive?

Solar power is no more expensive than running a generator. The value of a low-maintenance solar system compared with an engine generator is obvious. There are no fuel costs, time-consuming maintenance, or engine to wear out. Once installed, a solar system costs nothing.

Besides, expense is relative. Purchasing energy equipment is determined by the watts output (volts x amps = watts). Select the charge voltage with consideration of the battery and the outside temperature where you require the most power. If it gets over 95°F daily, select a panel with 36 solar cells. Where the weather is milder, you can get away with 33 cells. For an extra margin of safety, select panels with plenty of amps and a working voltage of 15 volts after the panel has warmed in the sunlight.

Does every RV need a solar panel whenever you're not in a park?
No. The RV battery is very durable. It can supply 12-volt power for a day or two without being recharged. An RVer who wishes to camp longer than a few days will need some method of recharge. Generator, solar, or vehicle alternators are available sources, each requiring some length of time to achieve full charge.

Do solar panels have to be kept in direct sunlight?
No, but the amps produced by panels are directly proportional to the intensity of the light (more light equals more power). Charging continues even on cloudy and overcast days.

I want to start with one panel and add on later. Is this OK?
Once the initial wiring system is installed, it takes only a few minutes to bolt the additional panels into place, and to connect the two wires. No added internal wiring is necessary.

What appliances will operate from one solar panel?
Solar panels for RVs are not intended to operate equipment directly. Their prime and *only* purpose is to recharge the 12-volt battery or batteries. So whatever appliances or equipment you operate from the battery can be used, with the solar panel(s) recharging the battery. How long you use the equipment and its amp draw then becomes the question.

Can I run a 12-volt hair dryer from one solar panel?
The solar panel only charges the battery. The battery supplies energy to the dryer, and the solar panel recharges the battery. This allows larger equipment to be used for short periods of time. It may

take several hours of sunlight on the panel to replace what was used in a short time because of the heavy draw.

How long can I operate my 2-amp light fixture and a 3-amp TV from the power generated by one solar panel?

Determine your average daily consumption of electricity. Make a list of equipment used, multiply the amp draw times the hours used to determine the ampere hours (AH). Add the totals for all devices used to get the daily requirement. For example: 4 hours of 2-amp light = 8 AH + 3 hours of 3-amp TV = 9 AH. Total 8 + 9 = 17 AH daily requirement. This 17 AH can be generated within the capability of a single 40- to 50-watt solar panel on an average clear day.

If I have one solar panel, what would be the advantage of having two of them?

Each solar panel supplies a certain amount of energy each day. For example, a 40- to 50-watt panel produces about 15 AH on a certain day. Having two panels would give you twice as much. If you use 25 AH per day, you need more than one day to refill your battery. Two panels would produce that in one day . . . and two panels charge twice as fast.

I have only one panel. What if I overuse my appliances to 40 AH in one day. Will I have enough power to use the following day?

The RV battery is like a bank account. You cannot take out more than you put in. If your account is full to start with, you may make heavy withdrawals while making smaller deposits. Conservation of use and knowledge of production will allow you to maintain a balanced battery system.

If I use a 5-inch TV (1 amp), 4 light bulbs, and a water pump (7 amps), how many panels will I need to recharge the battery?

To answer this question, I need to know how long each appliance will be used to determine the total AH required. The quality of sunlight is also a determining factor to how much energy each panel will generate.

I camp full-time without hook-ups, run my generator 4 hours a day, use an average of 38 AH daily. How many panels will I need to maintain my batteries in top shape?

Two 40- to 50-watt panels will serve your needs most of the year. During the winter months, you may need to supplement the charge level by driving (alternator), running the generator occasionally, or by cutting back (conservation) to meet your demands.

Is a solar panel's power used up with time?

Solar panels do not lose their ability to produce power. There are no moving parts, nothing to wear out. Leaving panels hooked up or open circuit makes no difference.

Can I still use the gasoline generator I paid so much for?

Most solar users never run their generators except for rare 120-volt uses. This extends engine life for when it is really needed.

Do solar panels have to be disconnected when driving?

No, there is no need to ever remove or disconnect the solar panels, even while charging the battery from another source.

Does freezing, heat or rain affect solar panels?

Solar panels are completely sealed, making them impervious to moisture. Cold temperatures actually make the panels work better. Hot weather reduces solar panel efficiency, so mounting frames must allow for air circulation.

Where can I mount panels? I only have a space 14-inches wide beside the A/C.

A single panel mounted beside the A/C might be shaded in winter. Use caution when placing panels in a tight space. All cells require illumination to be effective. Single panel mounts are available.

If I buy a new trailer, will it be difficult to reinstall my panels?

Solar electric systems are easy to move from one RV to another. Sealing a few holes and removing the wires takes only a few minutes. Save your installation guide for reinstallation ease.

I plan to keep my solar panels flat, and I don't plan to get on the RV roof. How many panels do I need?

The season (the angle of the sun) and your 12-volt usage dictate the balance and number of panels you need. Assuming your electrical needs in December, January, and February are the same as in the summer, you may run low on power during the winter. The solution: Add an extra panel, or use occasional back-up charging during these months. At other times of the year, panels remain flat.

I was considering the purchase of a "self-regulating" solar panel. Will it charge as well as other panels?

Self-regulating solar panels that have 30 solar cells are excellent for direct applications, such as operating pumps, but not so good for battery charging. In a fully operational RV these panels lack sufficient voltage to provide adequate charge when the weather is warm. Granted, they are cheaper than standard panels, and generally won't overcharge a battery, but since they don't have a regulator or diode, they can boil a battery dry on an unused system. The "self-regulating" mechanism employs three less cells to keep the cost down, but since they don't do the job, it doesn't matter what they cost. Keep in mind that any panel will be "self-regulating" if you carefully balance the power produced with the power consumed and the storage capacity of the battery bank. If you want to go through that exercise, good luck.

Do I need a voltage regulator?

A regulator is not necessary to charge batteries from solar panels. But when batteries become "full," it is desirable to turn off the charge (just like the regulator on your automotive battery). While a manual switch may be used, you may forget to turn the system "on" and "off." Regulation can also be achieved by having more batteries than the number of panels; they thus absorb the extra energy without harm. A regulator offers automatic operation, diode protection, and often includes meters for system monitoring.

I have a large 8-D battery with 1100 amps. Is this equal to 10 105-AH sized batteries?

On the contrary, the 8-D battery has a cold cranking amp (CCA) rating of 1100 amps. This is a measured ability to turn a starter and is not related to "capacity"—AH or reserve minutes ratings. (For capacity comparisons, one 8-D equals 208 AH is equivalent to two 105-AH batteries.) An 8-D is a heavy-duty unit, but is not of deep-cycle design.

Where can I situate an extra battery if I have no outside compartments?
Consider placing a completely sealed battery under the kitchen sink or under a dinette seat. Always heed safety precautions.

Can an RV alternator be overloaded by too many batteries?
Not really, but an automotive alternator only operates up to its maximum amp rating. While it warms up, that maximum is reduced by about 20%. As the batteries fill, the regulator cuts the charge rate back to a trickle. The top 30% of fill is slow going.

2
UNDERSTANDING ELECTRICITY

Knowing all there is to know about electricity is impossible. It is also unnecessary to the understanding of 12-volt DC (12VDC) systems for RV use. The basic electrical terms used throughout the book are defined here; other terms and concepts will be introduced as needed. When you have read through the glossary, you'll probably find you know a lot more about electricity than you thought.

Alternating Current (AC): Electric current which reverses its direction of flow many times per second; measured in cycles or hertz (Hz). Common usage is utility power: 120 volt AC, 60 cycles (Hz) per second. AC power cannot be stored. A converter will change AC to a rectified form of DC for battery storage.

Ampere (amp): Standard unit of measurement for rate of flow (current) in an electrical circuit. 1000 milli-amps (MA) = 1 amp. Amps are critical to the self-sufficient RVer who must produce the maximum number while consuming the minimum.

Ampere Hour (amp hour; AH): Number of amps produced or consumed in one hour. A current of 1 amp running for 1 hour = 1 AH. Note: Batteries are rated in AH—meaning the discharge capacity of a battery in a specified time, *not* amps per hour.

Example: An appliance that draws 5 amps for 1 hour uses 5 AH. If it does this once per day, it consumes 5 AH per day. If the same 5-amp load were to run for 24 hours, it would use 120 AH (5 × 24 = 120)—more energy than a battery holds.

Circuit: The path of an electric current. A closed circuit for our purposes—meaning a closed loop—connects supply, wires, and load. Series and parallel circuits will be discussed later.

Conductor: A single wire with insulation. A cable is composed of more than one conductor bound within a covering.

Current: Measured in amps, the flow of electrons through a conductor.

Direct Current (DC): Electric current that always flows in the same direction—negative to positive. A constant flow of electricity, this is the type of current produced by solar panels and batteries. An inverter is a device that converts DC power to AC power.

Efficiency: A percent value of comparison of power input to power output, determined by dividing energy out by energy in.

Load: Any equipment—appliance, light, or motor—that resists or receives electric current for use.

Resistance: Opposition to the free flow of electric current—anything that reduces electrical pressure (volts).

Volt (V): The unit of measure for electrical pressure.

Watt (W): The unit for measuring electrical energy or "work." Watts = amps × volts. If only two of the three values are known, you can determine the other algebraically. (1 horsepower = 746 watts.)

HOW ELECTRICITY WORKS

Electrons are negatively charged particles which flow along a wire (or conductor). They flow only when a complete circuit of conduction is present. This flow of electricity depends on pressure (volts) to make it travel the circuit.

Visualize a water hose connected together to form a circle, and connected to a pump. To circulate the water around and around, the pump requires only a small amount of energy. However, if a kink forms in the hose, resistance is created and the flow of water is slowed. In this analogy, the pump supplies the pressure (volts), and the kink is the load (resistance) which determines the flow (amps) of water.

Battery Storage and Recharge

Since batteries are covered in chapter 3, we will address the subject only briefly here.

Batteries are the only devices that can store direct current for later use. A battery is "refilled" from an outside source (solar cells, driving, etc.). As it fills, a resistance develops that pushes against the charging voltage. Recharging the battery is like filling a tank—eventually it will hold no more. Overcharge, as well as undercharge, is to be avoided, and the recharge rate must be kept low. A **regulator** automatically adjusts the charging current when the battery is full. Batteries must not be allowed to discharge fully.

Battery: A rechargeable electric storage unit that operates on the principle of changing electrical energy into chemical energy by means of a reversible chemical reaction. The lead-acid automobile battery is the most common example. Throw-away batteries are not rechargeable.

Battery Capacity: Rated in AH, the total amount of electricity that can be drawn from a fully charged battery until it is discharged to a specific voltage. A battery rated at 105 AH theoretically would deliver 105 amps for 1 hour, but realistically will deliver only 5 amps for 21 hours. A battery's state-of-charge is its available capacity, stated as a percentage of its rated capacity.

Battery Charger: A device which moves electrons from the battery's plates into the electrolyte—for example, an AC rectifying device, generator, or solar panel. It is this exchange of electrons between plate and electrolyte that releases the energy.

A battery charging source must have a higher voltage than the standing battery pressure. A typical solar panel, for example, produces 16 volts and so has the pressure to overcome the resistance of a 12-volt battery and will move electrons to the battery for storage.

Be very careful around batteries. Heed all the precautions given in chapter 3 and follow all instructions.

Circuits

A power source produces electrical pressure which causes current to flow through a circuit. The circuit must be complete in order for the electrons to flow. Remember, electrical pressure is called **voltage** which causes **current** (amps) to flow through a wire **conductor** to the **load** (resistance), then back to the **source** (generator). Figure 2.1 demonstrates this principle with an RV battery and lamp. The battery pressure (12 volts) pushes current (2 amps) through the lamp (load). Both connections (+ and −) are necessary for the current to flow. Measuring the flow of amps over a period of one hour is expressed as amp hours (AH). Here, the 2-amp lamp used for 3 hours = 6 AH. A **switch** breaks the circuit by cutting off electron flow.

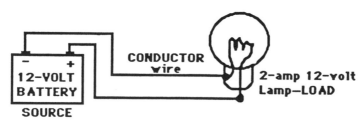

CONDUCTOR wire

− + 12-VOLT BATTERY

SOURCE

2-amp 12-volt Lamp—LOAD

FIGURE 2.1: How a circuit works.

Series Circuit: A circuit which affords only one path for the current to flow (see Figure 2.2). Batteries arranged in series are connected by the negative terminal of the first to the positive terminal of the second, the negative of the second to the positive of the third, and so on. If two 6-volt batteries are connected in series, the circuit voltage doubles to 12 volts.

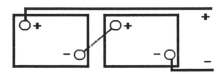

FIGURE 2.2: Series circuit. When batteries are connected in series, current remains constant and voltage increases.

Parallel Circuit: A circuit which provides more than one path for current flow (Figure 2.3). In a parallel arrangement, the positive terminal of one battery is connected to the positive terminal of the next, and the negative terminals are likewise connected. Voltage remains constant, but the amps double.

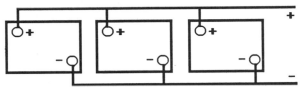

FIGURE 2.3: Parallel circuit. When batteries are connected in parallel, voltage remains constant and current increases.

Measuring, Testing, and Monitoring Devices

Visualize the water pump and hose again. While we can see water, we see only the effects of electricity via a lamp, motor, heater, appliance, or **meter**. Meters indicate amperes (flow) or volts (pressure), and so lets us "see" how our system is performing. Commonly used meters are described below. All are available as individual add-ons, but the meters you need for a solar system are also available as a control package with a regulator (see page 77).

Ammeter: Indicates the output in amps from the charging source. In the analog type, as opposed to a digital ammeter, the needle is moved by a magnetic field—the greater the current, the more movement.

Voltmeter: Shows the battery's state-of-charge. A digital or expanded-scale voltmeter is necessary to measure the minute voltage changes that occur in a battery from "full" to "empty." A voltmeter with positive and negative indicator leads (e.g., a portable voltmeter) can also be used to verify polarity.

Ohmmeter: Establishes continuity of a circuit and gives an ohm value to its resistance.

Multimeter: Combination system containing a voltmeter, ammeter, and ohmmeter.

Hydrometer: Differs from the above meters. This device shows the battery's state-of-charge by measuring the sulfate content of the battery's electrolyte. A hydrometer gives a specific gravity reading by means of a float indicator. Its use as a battery maintenance tool is described in chapter 3.

Inverters and Converters

Alternating current cannot be stored: It must be converted to direct current for storage. An advantage of AC is that it may be stepped up or down by a transformer. Voltage may be increased while the current is reduced proportionately. Transformers work on the principle of alternating magnetism and thus are not usable for DC, which does not "alternate," except when switched on or off.

An **inverter** (see chapter 7) changes battery power (DC) to AC, and then steps it up to 120VAC through a transformer. (But transformers don't work on DC! Electronic switching devices, however, will pulsate DC so that it appears as AC to the transformer.)

Conversely, a **converter** (i.e, battery charger, see chapter 3) reduces 120VAC to 12VDC in a transformer, and then eliminates the "alternations" to produce a direct current.

SOLAR ELECTRICITY

The phenomenon of changing sunlight directly into electricity via solar cells is an elegant process. The mechanical operation of solar systems is actually less complicated than that of conventionally powered generators.

Solar cells are made from wafers or sheets of silicon and then assembled into sealed solar panels. Appendix A contains a brief discussion of solar cells, the different types available, and how they are manufactured. For those who want even more technical information about the process, we refer you to *Practical Photovoltaics* by Dr. Richard Komp (see Appendix B).

Here, we will be talking about solar panels and their high efficiency and stability even under poor lighting and weather conditions—conditions likely to be encountered by the RVer.

Solar Panels—What They Do

Contrary to the popular belief that solar cells use the heat of the sun to make electricity, it is the wave or photo energy of sunlight that is converted to power. Solar cells, then, work anywhere the sun shines—not just where it's hot. Like a pump, the panel moves electrons through wires back into the battery and causes the recharge. That is all it does. Many RVers use solar panels as their sole means of battery recharging for powering lights, TV, and water pumps. Other replace their fuel generators with solar panels to supply extra energy for 120VAC inverter-supplied equipment. For others, solar trickle chargers maintain their batteries while the RV is in storage. In each case, the solar panels act only to recharge the battery.

Solar Panels—How They Work

In a typical solar panel, 32 to 36 solar cells are connected in series. The series and parallel circuit principles illustrated earlier for batteries apply here as well. The series connection of solar cells increases output voltage while current remains constant, and the parallel connection increases current while voltage remains constant (Figure 2.4). Whereas the panels we will be discussing are composed of series-connected solar cells, the solar panels themselves can be connected in parallel to increase current.

FIGURE 2.4: Solar cells of the same watt power arrangement can be connected in two ways. Solar cells connected in series (top) increase voltage, while a parallel connection increases current.

The current (amps) produced by a solar cell is proportional to the amount of light falling on its surface (Figure 2.5). So current increases with the surface area of the cell, as well as with the intensity of light. (On a cloudy day, a solar panel will produce power proportional to the light intensity: 50% light equals 50% power). A 4-inch solar cell, or a panel of 4-inch cells in series, produces about 3 amps at peak light. Two such panels connected in parallel increase the current to 6 amps.

Voltage remains constant at about 0.5 volt per cell regardless of the surface area. But connected in series, the output voltage is increased to exceed battery voltage to "push" the charge into a battery. Since 10 solar cells in series produce 5 volts, a panel of 32 or more cells will supply the voltage required to charge a 12-volt battery.

Panel voltage varies with ambient temperature, however (see Figure 2.6.) As ambient temperature increases, voltage decreases, and so the cooler the climate, the higher the output voltage. For example, an individual solar cell at 80°F generates approximately

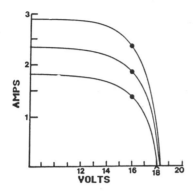

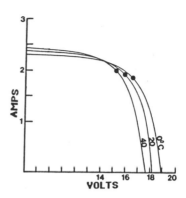

FIGURE 2.5: Current (amps) increases proportionally to the availability and intensity of light on a solar cell.

FIGURE 2.6: Panel voltage decreases with increasing ambient temperature.

0.49 volts. A solar panel with 33 solar cells would charge up to 16.2 volts (33 × 0.49 V). A solar panel positioned on the roof of an RV can easily reach 150°F on a hot day. At this temperature, the output voltage of an individual cell will reduce to 0.42, and so the same 33-cell panel would then charge only about 14 volts.

A successful solar system contains panels of 32 to 36 cells that can maintain at least 14 volts even when the climate is hot, normally operating in the 15 to 16 volt range. If you have fewer than 32 cells, you might not have sufficient voltage to achieve full charge. And if your panel has more than 36 cells, you might be paying for more cells than you need—anything beyond 16 working volts is wasted, unless you spend extended periods in especially hot climates. For the average RVer, a panel of 32 to 36 solar cells is optimal for year-round battery charging.

A solar panel is attached to a battery in a parallel connection: positive poles to positive and negative to negative. As electrons from both the panel and the battery attempt to travel around the circuit, the high panel voltage (16 volts) overcomes the resistance of the battery voltage (12 volts). Thus, the electrons move toward the battery and recharge takes place (Figure 2.7).

A Note on Reverse Flow

At night, or whenever there is no light on the solar panel, no voltage is produced. If allowed to remain "unchecked" in this state, the battery pushes a slow flow of electrons back through the panel, opposite to the charge direction. This reverse flow of current is small, about 55 MA per panel, but can add up during long winter nights or periods of bad weather—especially if you have multiple panels. For example, four panels × 55 MA = 220 MA (0.25 amp) × 16 hours = 4 AH per day. This amount of power loss could discharge your battery. The solution to reverse flow is a **diode** (Figure 2.8), which serves as an electrical check valve by limiting

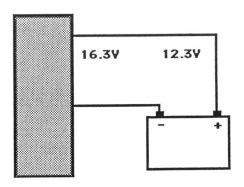

FIGURE 2.7: Solar panel voltage is higher than battery voltage. Net results, 4-volt difference, causes battery recharge to occur.

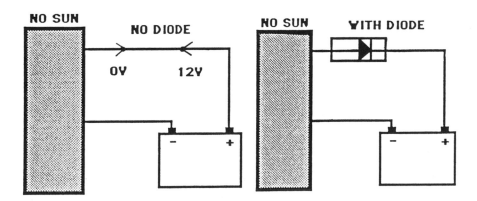

FIGURE 2.8: A diode prevents power loss due to reverse flow at night.

the flow of current to one direction. This prevents the loss of power "out" through the panel at night. Most regulators designed for solar use have a built-in diode.

Solar panels are ideal for RV battery charging. In the chapters ahead we will examine many of the less technical but equally important system characteristics—and the why and how-to. But first we'll examine the RV battery itself and some conventional charging sources.

3
BATTERIES AND CONVENTIONAL CHARGING METHODS

The heart of the RV electrical system is the storage battery. Batteries come in various sizes, shapes, and capacities, but all have one thing in common—they store DC current for later use, when the engine isn't running or the sun isn't shining. Batteries allow us to use large amounts of power for short periods of time, more than an engine alternator or a solar panel could produce during the same period.

The battery is often the least understood component of the RV electrical system. Admittedly, it is the weakest link, not only in a solar system but in any charging system. A battery will wear and eventually fail, but how it is used—or abused—affects its reliability and determines its life expectancy.

THE LEAD-ACID BATTERY

The lead-acid automotive/RV battery was developed nearly 100 years ago. Although refined and improved for reliability and low maintenance, the technology remains basically unchanged. When you start an RV engine or turn on the lights, the battery releases "chemical bound" electric current. Within the battery, a negative and a positive electrode made of lead and lead peroxide, respectively, are suspended in a power mixture of water and sulfuric acid called the electrolyte. When the circuit is activated and current flows, a new material, lead sulfate, accumulates in both battery plates (Figure 3.2).

FIGURE 3.1:
Battery components.

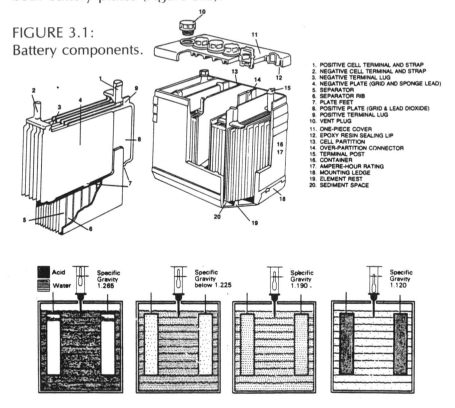

1. POSITIVE CELL TERMINAL AND STRAP
2. NEGATIVE CELL TERMINAL AND STRAP
3. NEGATIVE TERMINAL LUG
4. NEGATIVE PLATE (GRID AND SPONGE LEAD)
5. SEPARATOR
6. SEPARATOR RIB
7. PLATE FEET
8. POSITIVE PLATE (GRID & LEAD DIOXIDE)
9. POSITIVE TERMINAL LUG
10. VENT PLUG
11. ONE-PIECE COVER
12. EPOXY RESIN SEALING LIP
13. CELL PARTITION
14. OVER-PARTITION CONNECTOR
15. TERMINAL POST
16. CONTAINER
17. AMPERE-HOUR RATING
18. MOUNTING LEDGE
19. ELEMENT REST
20. SEDIMENT SPACE

FIGURE 3.2: Chemical changes that occur within the battery from a fully charged state through discharge.

As you use (discharge) the energy from your battery, the electrolyte weakens and the plates become heavily encrusted with lead sulfate. Recharging reverses this chemical reaction; current is forced back into the battery and the plates are restored to their original composition.

Theoretically a battery's discharge/recharge cycle should go on forever. However, since we have all replaced a battery or two, we know this is not the case. Each deep discharge washes some of the active lead material from the plates, a process called **shedding.** The deeper the discharge cycle, the greater the shedding.

In chapter 2 we stated that **battery capacity** is the total amount of electricity that can be drawn from a fully charged battery until it is discharged to a specified battery voltage. Battery capacity is rated in ampere hours (AH). A 100-AH battery can deliver 1 amp for 100 hours, or in practice 5 amps for 20 hours. **Available battery capacity** is a function of the battery's discharge rate. Figure 3.3 illustrates this relationship. Note the reduced capacity at various discharge rates. If the discharge rate exceeds the 20-hour rate, the battery will have less effective AH availability.

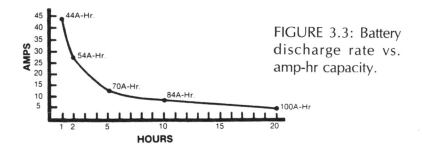

FIGURE 3.3: Battery discharge rate vs. amp-hr capacity.

A battery's **state-of-charge** is a measure of its available capacity and is stated as a percentage of its rated capacity. Actually it is the measurement of the sulfate content of the battery's electrolyte and can be ascertained by using a hydrometer or a voltmeter. Procedures for using these tools will be described later in this chapter (see "Analyzing, Testing, and Monitoring Your RV Battery").

While the output voltage of each battery cell depends on a number of factors (temperature, state-of-charge), we will use 2 volts. The total battery voltage is the sum of the individual cell voltages, so a battery with 3 cells in series is called a 6-volt battery, while a 12-volt battery has 6 cells in series. It is important to our discussion of 12-volt batteries to understand the differences between the two basic designs: **automotive** (starting) and **deep-cycle**.

Automotive Batteries

An automotive starter battery delivers a brief surge of power to start an engine and then receives an immediate rapid recharge by way of the alternator. It is constructed with thin plates and porous oxidizers to expose a maximum amount of active material to the electrolyte. This combination produces a lot of electrical energy but it can't withstand total discharge. If you leave your headlights on overnight, the battery will be completely discharged. Even though adequate function can usually be restored through recharge, some degree of permanent damage is inflicted each time complete discharge occurs.

A cycle is the complete sequence of battery operation: A fully charged battery is "emptied" of its power and then recharged or "filled up" again. The typical automobile battery is designed to tolerate a specific number of cycles over its lifetime and may lose as much as 50% of its capacity after being drained and recharged only 20 times.

Deep-Cycle Batteries

A deep-cycle battery can withstand repeated cycles of deep discharge—literally hundreds—and still function. In contrast to its automotive counterpart, a deep-cycle battery supplies a relatively low amount of current but over a prolonged period of time.

Differences in lead-acid batteries lie basically in the quality and amount of the lead plate material incorporated in construction. A deep-cycle battery (Figure 3.4) is constructed with thick lead

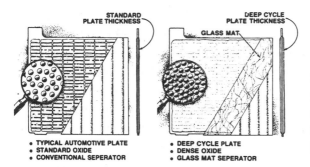

FIGURE 3.4: Construction differences of standard automotive and deep-cycle batteries.

plates and glass mat separators that inhibit shedding. Its greater electrolyte capacity increases reliability under difficult operating conditions. The electrolyte remains "close" to the plates, and the heavy construction protects against potential damage (such as that caused by RV vibration).

A deep-cycle battery weighs more and costs more than an automotive battery, but it also lasts much longer in an RV application. Life expectancy of about 200 deep cycles is typical—a lot of travel for the average RVer. Prompt recharge, especially the continuous, gentle charging afforded by a solar system extends deep-cycle battery life substantially.

BATTERY SELECTION

The proper selection of batteries is essential to achieving satisfactory results. Deep-cycle batteries are recommended for RV living even if you don't use solar power. If you have an inverter, the proper battery is especially important. RV/marine, trolling, golfcart, electric vehicle, and industrial-grade heavy-duty batteries are all well-suited to RV use.

Size and weight are obvious factors in battery selection because of space limitations and the need for ease of handling. Batteries are given manufacturers' designations according to size, e.g., group 24, group 27, etc. The more "active lead" in a battery, the higher its AH rating and the heavier its weight. Group 27 deep-cycle batteries measure about 13x7x9 inches, weigh about

55 pounds each, and are rated at 100 to 105 AH. The smaller lighter group 24 batteries are rated at 70 to 65 AH.

Some new batteries bear a "reserve minutes" rating rather than an AH rating. This rating is based on a test that determines how many minutes a new, fully charged battery can supply a 25-amp discharge before the voltage drops to 10.5 volts. The test, run at 80°F, is comparative only. In actual use it must be remembered that batteries that are discharged slowly give more power than those discharged quickly, and that temperature creates variations also (see "Temperature Effects").

A 160-minute reserve is considered a good rating for a group 27 battery. To calculate the AH rating from the reserve rating on these new batteries, multiply the reserve capacity by 0.6. For example, 160 reserve capacity × 0.6 = 96 AH.

The cold cranking amps (CCA) or "starting amps" listed for a battery have no relation to storage capacity. If the battery will be used for engine starting, especially for a V-8 or diesel engine, choose one with a high CCA rating, e.g., 450 to 500+. Some deep-cycle batteries with high reserve capacities may not have the good CCA ratings of heavier, more expensive ones. Self-sufficient RVers have discovered that using two to four deep-cycle batteries and easily achieving full charge with solar panels assures good starting power and long storage life.

Table 3.1 compares various battery ratings. In our experience, the most versatile battery for the average RVer is the group 27 RV/marine, which provides a good compromise between maximum reserve capacity and starting ability. It is also easy to handle and available just about anywhere at a comparatively low cost.

Table 3.1: Comparison of RV/Marine Deep-Cycle Battery Ratings

Size/Type	Capacity (AH)	Reserve (min)	CCA	Weight (lb)
Group #27	105	170	550	55
Group #24	70	110	420	42
8-D (truck)	240	380	900	120
Golfcart	220	350	470	130

New to the U.S., the Prevailer Gel battery, designed by Sonnonshine Germany, deserves special mention. A 62-pound group 27 battery with dual-purpose design for both starting and deep-cycle use, the Prevailer is rated to last longer than any other group 27 deep-cycle battery. It is also completely sealed, maintenance-free, and, because of its leakproof construction, can be used inside the RV coach in any position.

Deep-cycle batteries are rated also by the number of complete cycles they can undergo in their lifetime: the greater the cycle rating, the longer the expected lifespan. To determine the most economical deep-cycle for the life of a given system, use this formula to compare those under consideration.

[Initial Price ÷ # of AH (24 hr rate)] ÷ # of cycles the battery is rated for = "Cost per AH Cycle"

When selecting a battery, price is not everything. Reliability and peace of mind are much more important to those who frequent beautiful backwood or desert sites far from the battery dealers. Your local dealer can offer immediate service and answer your questions. National brands like Delco, GNB, J. C. Penneys, Sears, Interstate, Prevailer, and Wards offer the security and convenience of warranty service nationwide.

TEMPERATURE EFFECTS

Temperature has a significant effect on battery capacity and performance. Staying within a range of 25 to 95°F is recommended. Low temperatures reduce available battery capacity (as illustrated in Figure 3.5.) At 80°F, the battery capacity is 100%, at 32°F it drops to 65%, and at 0°F it reduces further to 40%.

Extreme temperature affects a battery's overall life expectancy as well. High temperatures—like those beneath the hood of an engine compartment—will shorten the life of a battery by accelerating the chemical reactions within the cells. At the opposite extreme, if a discharged battery (that is, one with weak electrolyte) is allowed to freeze, irreversible damage results. It is important to locate storage batteries so to minimize the effects of temperature.

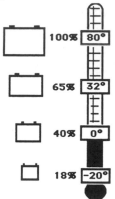

FIGURE 3.5: Power available from battery (percent) at normal and low temperatures.

SULFATION, AGING, AND SELF-DISCHARGE

Sulfation results naturally to some degree each time a battery discharges. When lead is converted to lead sulfate it more than coats both plates, it actually impregnates them. If not reversed by recharging, sulfation can destroy the porosity of the plates and thereby a battery's ability to produce power. In its initial stage, sulfate is "soft" and nondestructive. Over time, though, it will harden into crystals that may be impossible to reverse.

Age affects a battery's ability to store and deliver its rated output. Shedding and sulfation are accumulative, and because a single weak or sulfating battery cell will render a battery ineffective, proper maintenance is important for prolonging cycle life. A battery which has gradually lost its capacity through aging will show a full charge more readily than a new battery. It also loses its ability to resist overcharge, and acid-laden vapors can pour out of the vents when in reality the battery is at 40% or less of original capacity. Don't be fooled by the fact that a sulfated battery will carry a surface charge, even enough to start your RV. A load tester at a battery shop can determine this elusive condition.

If a battery is allowed to stand unused and uncharged for a long period of time, **self-discharge** will result in sulfation. Self-discharge results from impurities within plate construction and from those induced by adding tapwater. About 5 to 30% (or 6% in a new lead-calcium battery) of a battery's capacity can be lost each month the battery remains idle; the self-discharge rate is even higher when a battery is left sitting in temperatures over 90°F. Chapter 5 describes a small, inexpensive solar trickle charger that can maintain your batteries while your RV is in storage.

If a battery has lost its charge due to self-discharge, or if sulfation has occurred, recharging will be difficult and sometimes impossible. The battery will never be able to hold a full charge again. Do not add acid to a sulfated battery—or to any battery, for that matter. The excess sulfate will lead to more crystal build-up, will slow recharge, and will also eat away the support grids. If a battery will not accept current when 15 volts are applied, it might as well be thrown away.

BATTERY COMPARTMENTS

Proper ventilation and insulation are essential considerations in battery placement. Some new, completely sealed batteries like the Stowaway do not require outside ventilation and can be safely placed under a kitchen cabinet, a table, or even a bed inside the RV. However, any RV battery with removable caps should be placed in a ventilated compartment. Ventilation protection against fumes and corrosion is particularly important in bus conversions and large "class A" RVs equipped with several large (8-D or golfcart) batteries that carry tremendous amounts of stored energy. Insulation should be sufficient to maintain a relatively uniform temperature and to protect batteries from the wide variations that reduce operating capacity and life expectancy.

If the typical, nonsealed battery is located anywhere other than in a specially designed compartment, it should be enclosed in a plastic battery case. The case keeps the battery in place, prevents acid spillage, and, most importantly, protects the terminals from accidental contact with metal objects that could cause sparks and fire.

FIGURE 3.6: A battery case installed behind propane tanks is limited in expansion potential. But a parallel connection to an additional battery in a custom compartment or to a sealed battery within the RV will double your capacity.

FIGURE 3.7: A typical tongue-mount for batteries. Note multiple connecting wires. Outside mounting has potential for dirt collection on battery.

Only essential wiring cables should have entry to the battery compartment. Do not locate the circuit distribution board and fuse panel within the compartment because corrosion to these components can lead to system failure. The main supply wires should be the soft, flexible type that can be secured to the wall and fed through a grommet-protected hole to prevent abrasion and potential short-circuits.

FIGURE 3.8: Batteries and inverters mounted in the same compartment. Note large wire battery hook-up and nice terminal block arrangement for corrosion-free connections.

RV manufacturers traditionally have allowed only minimal space for battery package placement (Figures 3.9 and 3.10). This is especially true in mini-motorhomes and van conversions where cramped battery quarters make it virtually impossible to check electrolyte levels without disconnecting several wires and physically removing the battery. Needless to say, a battery in such a location will not be serviced very often.

FIGURE 3.9: A good-sized battery compartment holds a group 27 battery. Note vent louvers and service space above cells.

FIGURE 3.10: This cramped battery compartment can accept only a group 24 battery. There is no room for expansion and no room for servicing.

A custom battery compartment (Figure 3.11) should include a strong, flat base for support, a noncorrosive lining, a dust seal around the opening, and easy service access to the tops of the battery cells. A single group 24 battery is just not large enough to sustain electrically independent camping for more than a couple of days, but with a little imagination and some help from a technician or mechanic, a suitable space for additional battery capacity can be found and developed. Pullout trays (Figure 3.12) offer easy access but can be difficult to seal if suspended beneath the RV chassis. A complete bottom and seal will protect against road dust and water. Some RVers create space by welding a bracket beneath the vehicle suspension with access through a trap door in the floor or side.

FIGURE 3.11: A custom battery compartment—insulated, dust-sealed, with easy service access.

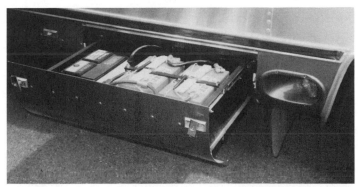

FIGURE 3.12: Convenient factory-built (top) and custom-built (bottom) battery pull-out trays.

Because of its modular construction, a solar system can be expanded easily. If you decide to install a one-panel "starter" system it would be wise to plan your battery compartment to allow for future additions. Planning ahead saves time and frustration later. Remember that batteries are inherently modular, too. You can just add more in parallel—if you have allowed sufficient space for expansion.

FIGURE 3.13: This custom battery box is rear bumper-mounted. Venting in tight-fitting lid keeps dirt and corrosion to a minimum. The inverter is situated inside the trunk.

BATTERY MAINTENANCE

Though an integral part of the electrical system, the battery is often overlooked when it comes to regular servicing. Hidden away in a compartment or mud-encrusted tray, with no interesting gadgets to adjust or gauges to monitor, it may elude your attention. But if you don't give the battery proper maintenance, that gleaming $80,000 RV won't be worth much to you. Good access to batteries is essential for observing their function and performing maintenance. A monthly battery checkup is time well spent and actually takes less time to perform than to describe. The following are suggested monthly procedures for all batteries except the sealed, maintenance-free types. It is worth the effort to take good care of your battery.

Warning: Exercise extreme caution when working with batteries. Batteries contain corrosive acid that not only will eat holes in your clothes, but can cause bad burns and blindness. Shield skin and wear goggles when servicing batteries. If acid should spill or splash on you, wash it off immediately with water. A baking soda/water solution will neutralize the acid.

Batteries give off explosive hydrogen fumes when charging and discharging. Keep sparks and flames away—and that includes cigarettes! An accidental spark or short-circuit could cause an explosion.

A metal object carelessly placed or dropped onto the battery terminals can cause major damage. Keep all tools in their proper places. And keep children away. Be careful!

1. Check electrolyte level on a monthly basis and add distilled water as necessary to indicated level. Tapwater contains minerals that reduce battery capacity and shorten its life. During hot weather some evaporation and electrolyte loss is normal, but if the electrolyte drops below the level of the plates, the exposed portion becomes less active.
2. Clean the tops of the batteries. Use a cloth dampened with water plus a little baking soda to neutralize the acid. Do not let baking soda get into the cells. Rinse with a cloth dampened with plain water and dry thoroughly. A mixture of moist electrolyte, dust, and corrosion on the case can cause self-discharge as a slow leakage of power across the output terminals.
3. Clean the battery terminals with a wire brush, and check and tighten connections for a secure fit. Good contact will ensure a full flow of electrical current. Corrosion can cause a disconnect by eating through metal wire and will act as an insulator that can also break the circuit. Prevent corrosion by cleaning and coating exposed metal connectors with a protective chemical, petroleum jelly, or silicone dialectric grease. To prevent corrosion from traveling up a wire and under the insulation, first heat the cleaned wire and then dip it in coating agent to seal.

4. Keep batteries charged to prevent sulfate formation and to extend battery life. An equalization charge every two to three weeks is recommended to balance a battery's cells in which sulfate deposits may accumulate. If the specific gravity reading of one or two cells is different from the others (see "Voltmeters and Hydrometers"), then slight overcharging of the battery will drive the sulfate build-up back into solution.

As its name implies, an **equalization charge** corrects inequalities that may exist among the cells. It is actually a gentle overcharge (about 5 amps) that should be administered up to 8 to 10 hours to equalize the electrolyte in each cell. A solar system accomplishes equalization charging automatically as the sun is setting.

Analyzing, Testing, and Monitoring Your RV Battery

Part of good battery maintenance is the regular testing of individual batteries, as well as whenever a problem is suspected. Checking out your entire charging system before a long trip and at the beginning of travel season is recommended practice and will save you the inconvenience and expense of electrical system failure far from home.

As explained earlier, temperature, age, and chemical composition will affect battery performance. One weak or sulfating cell can cause total ineffectiveness, and while a regular voltmeter reading might appear satisfactory, your battery may not hold up under load. Have your batteries tested on a battery analyzer, and use your voltmeter and hydrometer to take regular readings. Keep a record of these readings for comparison purposes.

Battery Analyzers

A battery analyzer, or load tester, can be found at any battery shop. A few dollars will buy you the most reliable appraisal of your battery's ability to deliver power. There is no better way to "look inside" a sealed or regular battery than to test it under load with the proper equipment. In fact it is the only way to test the newer sealed batteries. This test should be administered every six months to detect and correct problems that can lead to system failure. Full-time RVers may want to purchase a portable battery analyzer from a battery shop or specialty electrical supplier.

Charge your battery fully before taking it to the shop for testing. The battery analyzer applies a 50+ amp load for a few seconds to remove the surface charge and then measures the voltage drop on its meter while the battery is under load. A color-coded meter indicates whether the battery is still useful or should be discarded.

If you suspect that a battery has lost capacity, a battery analyzer can confirm this condition for you. This problem, usually due to aging, abuse, or manufacturing defect, can occur even in a relatively new battery. If your 105-AH battery indicates "full" voltage at about 14.5 volts very soon after you begin charging and then drops rapidly when you use just a small amount of power, it probably has lost capacity. A voltmeter reading of more than 0.5-volt drop (resting to under-load voltage) while using 10 to 15 amps means you need to replace your battery.

Voltmeters and Hydrometers

You wouldn't start out on a cross-country trip without knowing how much fuel you had. You make it a point to know. When the gauge reads 1/4-full, you start looking for a filling station. The same is true with batteries. You need to keep track of the numbers to avoid running out of battery power.

The voltmeter measures your battery's state-of-charge. A high-quality voltmeter is essential for detecting the minute voltage line differences that occur in 12-volt systems. A 50% capacity of change approximates only 0.6 volt—undetectable on the general purpose meters available at automotive stores. Even when using a large 3-inch meter, there is only about 1/16-inch to indicate each volt. This makes it almost impossible to differentiate between 12 and 12.5 volts. This 0.5-volt difference can indicate up to 50% of your battery bank's capacity. From the "resting" (no load, no charging) voltage of 11.5 volts (0%, dead) to 12.7 volts (100%, full) is only a little over 1 volt—also difficult to discern. Expanded-scale and digital voltmeters (Figure 3.14) are accurate and easy to read. For solar systems, an expanded-scale voltmeter is built-in as part of a prepackaged control center that houses the regulator and am-meter (see page 77).

Whereas a voltmeter allows you to take quick, easy readings of your battery state-of-charge as a percentage value, a hydrometer measures the amount of sulfuric acid in the electrolyte and gives you a specific gravity reading. Normally, each cell in a battery is within a few points on the scale of its companion cells. High specific gravity means that the battery is near full charge. A low specific gravity reading is the first sign of sulfation, and a hydrom-eter can detect a weak or sulfating cell before it becomes a serious problem by comparing each cell to the others.

We have used several types of hydrometers. The glass tube-type with graduated floats (Figure 3.15) are accurate but can be difficult to read, as are the large professional hydrometers with temperature-compensated scales. Floating ball hydrometers don't

FIGURE 3.14: Expanded-scale or digital voltmeters are more accurate than RV color-coded "battery condition meters" that can mislead by reading "good" as your TV screen image begins to shrink.

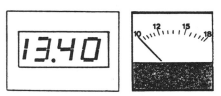

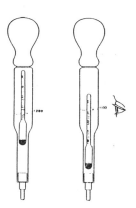

FIGURE 3.15: A hydrometer with graduated float gives numerical readings of specific gravity. In the floating ball hydrometer, a bat-tery is fully charged with all four balls afloat. If three float, you have 75%; if only one or two float, your battery is depleted.

give numerical readings but are easy to read and give reliable values for comparison (by the number of balls that float in the electrolyte drawn from the battery cells). Take hydrometer readings on a regular basis, monthly or bimonthly, during regular maintenance checks. Don't take readings immediately after adding water to a cell. A reading taken after prolonged cranking will be higher than true.

If you compare voltmeter and hydrometer readings, as illustrated in Table 3.2, you will see that very small changes in specific gravity represent major changes in state-of-charge.

Table 3.2: State-of-Charge by Specific Gravity and Voltmeter Readings

Specific Gravity	Voltmeter Reading	State-of-Charge
1.270	12.7	100%
1.250	12.5	75%
1.190	12.3	50%
1.150	12.1	25%
1.120	11.8	Discharged

BATTERY CHARGING PRINCIPLES AND CONVENTIONAL CHARGING SOURCES

The RV is a marvelous invention—a house on wheels with kitchen, bedroom, and bath. Some rigs are spacious while others are compact, but every RV depends on a reliable electrical supply from the battery. A utility hook-up for 120VAC appears to be the least expensive power source per kilowatt-hour, but the cord defeats the concept of RV independence and those park fees do add up. A tow vehicle, when underway, can be a battery charging source for a trailer. The motorhome, an integral unit, usually relies on a large built-in engine generator along with the automotive alternator for its electricity. No matter what the source, proper charging is essential to battery performance and life. Some basic principles must be kept in mind.

- Recharge the battery as soon as possible after use, and recharge it fully. If a battery is less than completely recharged each time it is used, it will become progressively less effective.
- Batteries respond best to a slow charge, e.g., between 3 and 10 amps. Fast charging from an outside source can be safely delivered only to the 75% fill level.
- Avoid discharging a deep-cycle battery to more than 40% of its capacity. In fact, using only the top 15 to 20% will prolong cycle life indefinitely.
- Avoid overcharging. It can cause overheating and structural damage within the battery.

A solar system achieves these charging parameters automatically. And, it may be restated, the amortized cost of a solar system is actually less than that of other charging options. The remaining chapters are devoted to the solar alternative. But because more than half of all vehicle problems are electrical, the RVer should understand the functions and limitations of the conventional RV charging system: automotive alternator, isolator, generator, and converter.

Automotive Alternators

The purpose of the automotive alternator, as intended by the manufacturer, is to charge the battery and furnish electrical accessories with enough current to operate while the engine is running. Driving to recharge the battery works great if you're on the road daily, but driving *just* to fill your battery is neither sensible nor economical.

Running the main engine equipped with its original 30- to 60-amp (or heavy-duty replacement 60-to 150-amp) alternator while traveling can charge the battery *if* the battery will accept the charge. Your alternator does not detect the number and size of batteries you are using—it merely senses their ability to receive current.

In addition to the number and size of batteries, other limiting charging factors to consider are: design output of the alternator, rpm, temperature of regulator and alternator, belt width/tension, connectors, isolators, and the distance and size of wire to batteries. If the battery is in a trailer 30 to 40 feet from the alternator, the distance itself reduces the amps that reach the battery.

Check your charging system! Secure connections are necessary for proper charging. An alternator that is not properly connected to a battery, or that has loosely wired or corroded connections, can leave you with a dead battery and a damaged alternator. Check for frayed or twisted wires at the alternator and restore them to orderly, full-thickness connections. A chassis ground is one area that can be overlooked. Also, a ground wire leading to appliances is essential for efficient operation.

A replacement heavy-duty alternator (available from Wrangler, TNT Electric or Lestek Manufacturing, Inc.) is an excellent investment for use with automatic energy-selecting refrigerators, dash air, multiple lighting, and other accessories which can draw up to 40 amps on the vehicle circuits. Recharging a depleted battery may require more than six hours driving time with all the other demands on the alternator.

Remember, the battery can only receive and store electrical energy—it cannot produce it. Keep in mind that it takes time to recharge a battery. A fast charge from a few minutes of driving is not sufficient to saturate the battery plate with electrons.

Isolators

An isolator (Figure 3.16) separates the auxiliary from the starting battery, preventing both from discharging while using the auxiliary battery. A solid-state mechanical solenoid or a manual switch can serve to separate the two electrical systems, at the same time allowing charge to each while the alternator is operating.

The solid-state isolator (diode) is an automatic device with the single disadvantage of a 0.5-volt drop which can limit the charging value. Sure Power Products, Inc. manufactures reliable isolators offered by many RV suppliers. Heat sink rating and adequate wire size are important factors in installation.

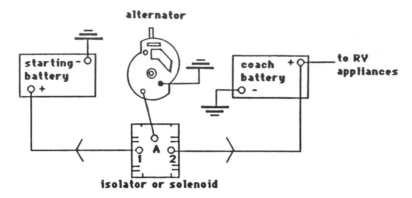

FIGURE 3.16: Isolators allow charge to go to both batteries, but does not allow the batteries to discharge from one to another.

Isolating a battery can also be accomplished by using a manual switch. While charging, the batteries will fill together without voltage restriction if the wires are of sufficient size for the current flow. The batteries will also *discharge* together unless the switch is manually operated. Cole-Hersee manufactures a good heavy-duty marine switch of use to the RVer.

Generators

Generators come in all sizes, from a handy 500-watt portable for operating small AC tools and appliances, to large diesel 12-kW units used in bus conversions. They all require manual operation and control, constant fuel handling, expensive maintenance, and parts replacement. Not to mention the noise and exhaust fumes that irritate and alienate your neighbors. Battery recharging through a generator is a slow process and impractical when using 1 to 2 gallons of fuel per hour. Today, better alternatives exist—especially for battery charging.

Engine generators, such as those available from Kohler and Onan, are useful during emergencies as back-up battery charging and when temporary power is needed for heavy or long-running loads. Refrigerators, welding equipment, and well pumps can overuse a battery/inverter system. And, of course, the big gas guzzlers are indispensable for running the roof air conditioners installed in most motorhomes.

Engine generators produce large quantities of electricity rapidly. When a generator is run at partial loading, however, inefficient operation and eventual damage results. Small convenience loads are better supplied by an inverter (see chapter 7). Save your generator from premature overhaul by using it for large essential loads.

Converters

Converters change 120VAC to 12VDC. Manufactured by B-W Manufacturers, Newmark Products, Progressive Dynamics, Inc., Triad-Utrad, and Univolt, converters supply power from the campground or generator to a host of low-voltage appliances while saving battery power. With slight variations, all converters contain a transformer to reduce the 120VAC to 12VDC, rectifiers to obtain direct current, fuses, and switches to direct the flow (see Figure 3.17). Converters use some power even while not supplying a load—feel the warm transformer and listen to it hum.

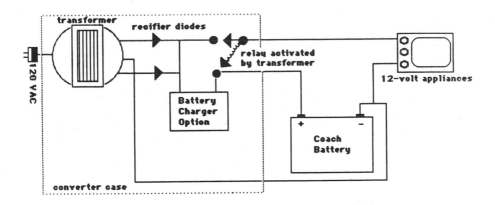

FIGURE 3.17: An RV converter consists of a transformer and a rectifier diode, with wiring connections from 120VAC to 12VDC loads as well as to the RV battery.

Some converters, while connected to 120VAC, also recharge the battery and prevent self-discharge. Converters supply on demand 30, 40, or 60 amps of 12-volt power and are rated accordingly, but for battery charging applications their fill rate may be less than 5 amps and reduces even further (0.5 amp or so) as the battery approaches 95% capacity. An ammeter in the battery charging line will usually show a fill rate of only 2.5 to 5 amps to the battery. So, while many people assume that a power converter is a rapid battery charger, in reality it is a good, slow "float trickle charger" that protects the battery from overcharge.

Using the generator in combination with the converter to recharge a low battery requires several hours or days of operation to obtain the desired fill—impractical and expensive. For a "fast charge" you probably could do better with an inexpensive automotive (Sears or K-Mart) or industrial (LaMarche or Solar brand) charger. And, rapid recharging (up to 65 amps) is possible with a high-quality standby inverter with built-in battery charger. These models are efficient and can be adjusted to your desired fill level.

If a problem arises with your power converter, more often than not the supply breaker is "off," the plug removed, the fuse blown, or a connection loose. Beyond checking the manufacturer's wiring diagram and instructions, any other problem should be left to a service technician with the proper test equipment.

To determine if your converter/charger is operating properly, connect it to a battery and make sure the AC power is on. Using a voltmeter to check battery outlet voltage without a battery attached will give a false reading—like 10 volts. The DC voltage with the converter on at the battery should show a reading of 13.5 to 13.9 when the battery is fully charged. The auxiliary battery condition is important for the converter to operate as a charger. When a battery indicates "full" to a voltmeter, then loses its charge rapidly, it is due to lost internal capacity—you need a new battery.

Because of the slow battery fill rate, technical problems, and the continuous 100-watt electric power consumption (much of the utility-purchased current being lost as heat), increasing numbers of RVers are disconnecting their converters and installing properly sized solar electric systems. They have discovered that a couple of solar panels can perform the same tasks reliably, without noise, without mechanical wear—and without fossil fuels.

4

USING SOLAR ELECTRICITY IN THE RV

You are your own power company! Using low-voltage power in your RV is different from and in many ways superior to a utility-connected system. Power company problems are no longer your problems. On the other hand, your problems are strictly your problems.

When parked at that secluded spot—away from crowded campgrounds, hook-ups, and noisy generators—you are dependent on yourself and your battery supply. Conserving that battery supply is of paramount importance. In fact, conservation is just good sense no matter where you live. Having an abundance is not a license to squander. In the contained world of RV living, the wise use of your resources is especially necessary. A basic understanding of your system's strengths and limitations will help you make intelligent decisions about using power effectively.

This chapter describes how low-voltage systems can meet your electrical needs for lighting, entertainment systems, appliances, tools, pumps, space heating and cooling, and refrigeration.

FIGURE 4.1: The solar panels mounted on this motorhome offer electrical independence for the 12-volt RV system.

It also advises as to their best, most efficient use. Together with the sizing information in chapter 5, this chapter will help you determine and meet your power requirements.

But first, a few comments from some RVers who are already enjoying the self-sufficiency of solar battery charging.

Dear Noel and Barbara—

We have enjoyed the freedom solar has given us since we got our two solar panels a few years ago. The entire solar system is operating perfectly—it's great for running our computer, satellite TV, and ham radio equipment.

Bill & Bobi Dawson
Nevada

We've been full-timing for three years now. Since getting solar on our motorhome two years ago, we have noticed how our RV friends separate themselves by method used for battery charging. The generator crowd can keep their generators way over there! Thought you might like to pass this on to RVers who want to enjoy the quiet peace of solar. See ya down the road.

John & Mable Carson
Kansas

We are glad to be full-time RVers in our 36-foot fifth-wheel rig. It has served us comfortably and is equipped with three solar panels, regulator/meter, inverter, two heaters, awning on refrigerator wall, and microwave oven. We save the 4000-watt generator for air conditioning. Having a ball in our retirement—we keep trying to see it all.

Ralph & Connie Janes
Oregon

We continue to enjoy our solar panels and are glad to be free from the electrical worry.

Joe & Mary Walden
Washington

Just to let you know, the four panels are working fine. I have four deep-cycle marine batteries and a 1000-watt inverter. Buying the inverter proved less expensive than getting all 12-volt appliances.

Wanda Schug
Colorado

LIGHTING

Lighting, usually taken for granted, is a primary user of electricity, especially in winter when days are shorter and we retire earlier to our RVs. An RV without proper lighting would be a dismal place, and the quality of light desired influences selection. Conservation can best be accomplished by choosing lights which give the most illumination for the least wattage. We can make an informed decision, weighing cost and quality of light, among the three options described below: incandescent, quartz halogen, and fluorescent lights.

Incandescent Lighting

The common automotive-type lamp (often called bulb) contains a filament wire that gets white-hot to emit light—and heat. This light has a warm quality, but several bulbs may be required to illuminate a large area. RV manufacturers install incandescent fixtures because they are the least expensive, but the heat they generate in use makes them the least efficient as well. Using incandescents in combination with fluorescents creates an effective lighting scheme.

When selecting lamps for 12-volt use, don't use the typical "tail light" types found in most RVs unless there is a reason. Consider the lamp's use and check the manufacturer's rating for amp draw, life, and candle power. Lamps #1487 and #1747 have less light output but longer life and can be used in areas where less light is needed.

Quartz Halogen Lighting

The filament of the quartz halogen bulb burns hotter and produces a whiter, brighter light than the incandescent bulb and gives 20 to 50% more light for the same wattage. Quartz halogen lights require special fixtures, adapters, and shields because their intensity can easily melt ordinary plastic and they can shatter under certain conditions. Quartz halogen lighting is very effective in work and reading areas, but the bulb/fixture expense is higher and lifespan shorter than other options.

Fluorescent Lighting

Fluorescent lights are coated vapor-filled tubes that generate very little heat while producing up to four times the light of incandescent bulbs. Selecting full-spectrum, warm-color hues from the variety of tubes available gives balanced skin tones which make people look and feel good. Fixtures are expensive, but the investment in a top-quality unit assures long-lasting performance (up to 2000 hours). We have found Thin-Lite by REC and Travellite by McLean Electronics to be reliable.

A 20-watt fluorescent tube produces about the same lumens as an 80-watt incandescent bulb when operated from a high-frequency DC ballast, which is more effective than a 120VAC ballast, offering unusually high efficiency. Furthermore, a two-tube fixture consumes about the same amount of electricity as a single incandescent bulb.

All fluorescent tubes are standard 120VAC used with high-efficiency ballasts, similar to a mini-inverter, which allows 12VDC operation. If you are considering inexpensive 120VAC fluorescent fixtures powered by an inverter, you may have problems. The quality of most 120VAC ballasts is poor compared to a 12VDC solid-state ballast, and the inverter will operate in its least-efficient power range, thereby causing that fluorescent to hum. Also, the induction load from a ballast is not always sufficient to keep an inverter activated to start lights properly. IOTA Manufacturing and Sunalux make very reliable high-efficiency DC ballasts, with a selection for any size tube, which are also very good at filtering out "noise" that interferes with radio and TV.

We do not recommend eliminating all incandescents in your RV. Rather, use a few strategically situated fluorescents and a number of single-bulb incandescents: fluorescents in main areas where lights are on for long periods, incandescents for direct-illumination reading or workplace lighting.

Other Lighting Tips

- Propane lights can supplement your overall scheme while helping to heat the RV.
- Remove the lens diffusers from fixtures to increase direct light output—but never remove the covers from quartz halogen lamps.
- Convert portable high-intensity desk lamps to operate on 12VDC. Check the bulb first. If it is 12-volt, the lamp can be modified easily. Open the base, cut the wires at the transformer and replace the AC cord or modify the end with a DC plug. Route and solder this wire through the switch. Reassemble the base leaving the disconnected transformer inside and you have a weighted desk lamp.

ENTERTAINMENT SYSTEMS

RVers are now accustomed to the gamut of home entertainment systems: 12VDC stereos, TVs, VCRs, and CB radios. Many 120VAC home stereos, tape decks, and turntables can be converted to 12VDC. Some RVers use inverters and 120VAC but at a decreased level of efficiency when compared to the quality 12VDC entertainment systems available today.

A small TV set is a good example of 120VAC versus 12VDC efficiency. Using 55 watts in the 120VAC mode, the same TV uses only 35 watts from 12VDC. The built-in AC/DC converter and transformer in the 120VAC model are responsible for the energy loss. Use the 12-volt adapter cord on entertainment systems where practical.

Color TV sets draw up to three times the power of black-and-white sets of the same size. Most folks who have color TV have two solar panels because of the extra power draw, and some maintain one color set and one black-and-white for convenience. Compare the amp ratings on at least three 12-volt color sets before you buy. Better is not necessarily more expensive. TMK and some other 9-inch color TVs draw only about 2 amps and are large enough for most RVers.

Satellite receivers are the new RV rage. The moderately priced models require manual assembly, mounting, and aiming—way too much trouble for us! Motorized roof-mounted models are still too expensive. Some require 120VAC, which necessitates the use of an inverter or generator for power supply.

Computers

For a computer/monitor/printer set-up, use a small-sized (300-watt) inverter with quality regulated power. (Voltage and frequency regulation is necessary for the best operation of electronics.) A computer run from an inverter becomes an uninterruptible power supply, unaffected by any of the problems utility power may experience.

Warning: To avoid crashes, do not run your computer while starting a large load.

FIGURE 4.2: A computer and workshop is run—via PV—in this customized van. (Courtesy A.D. Paul Wilkins, Solar Works!)

INVERTERS, 12-VOLT APPLIANCES, DC CONVERSIONS

Inverters (covered in chapter 7) are practical for small appliances and tools used for short periods. They offer 24-hour convenience without after-hours noise and allow the use of devices that are difficult to convert or to obtain as 12-volt models. In some cases it is cheaper to buy an inverter than to replace appliances, and if you have just a couple of favorites, you may need only a low-wattage, inexpensive inverter.

Shop around and check the energy efficiency on any 12-volt electrical equipment before you buy. Appliances used for longer periods—lights, fans, radios, TVs, and bed warmers—can consume more than their share of battery-stored reserves. Hidden loads are built-in on some modern RVs: gas/smoke detectors, digital clocks, computers, and electronic brains. The small amounts of 12-volt power required 24 hours per day adds up and can drain your battery if you are parked for a week or so. Amp draws for commonly used RV appliances are listed in the sizing section of chapter 5.

Appliances with heating elements use lots of amps fast! Choose one that does the job quickly, but be wary. One currently

marketed 160-watt, 12-volt clothing iron just doesn't work—
except on silk neckties. In a case like this, low amp draw is not the
deciding factor.

Small 12-volt automobile vacuums are inexpensive and
handy in the kitchen or workshop, but are not designed for large
carpeted areas. Standard 120VAC vacuum cleaners will work from
a 1000-watt inverter.

A 12-volt fry pan or coffeemaker draws about 14 amps. They
are usual cheaply made and are not recommended. A good 12-volt
blender that has been used successfully by many RVers is available
from Camping World.

Makita offers professional-quality rechargeable saws and
drills. Many standard tools can be modified for recharging from
your 12-volt RV system. Michael Hackleman's *Better Use of . . .
Electricity* (see Appendix B) is highly recommended as the best
in-depth reference available and offers modification instructions.

The large surplus of industrial DC motors that exists means
that many tools can be run directly from batteries. Retrofitting a
belt-driven sewing machine or rock tumbler is simple. Belt and
pulley drives are especially suited for replacing several motors with
one by using a "cradle-motor tension mount." Windlight Workshop offers a full selection of high-efficiency motors for DC
conversions.

Rechargeable and ni-cad batteries (sizes AA, C, and D) can be
recharged many times. Each charge lasts only about half as long as
a common dry-cell battery, but you will often get 50 times the
battery life for each dollar spent. Ni-cad batteries are not effective
in cold conditions, though, and must be discharged completely
before recharging.

Most RVs have at least one 12-volt receptacle, often called a
"cigarette lighter socket." These outlets are *not* designed to withstand the heat of a lighter, however. When installing additional
outlets, be sure to use heavy #12 or #10 wire on a fused circuit.

WATER SYSTEM

The typical demand water pump draws about four to eight amps while running. Because it runs only a few minutes each day, the amount of power consumed is negligible unless a malfunction (for example, a dry pumped tank) occurs.

Adding a precharged accumulator tank in the cold water line offers pressurized water for two or three gallons of draindown before the pump cycles. If you turn off your pump at night, you will still have running water without running the pump—and you'll save power and switch wear. We do not recommend the small plastic accumulators sold by RV pump manufacturers, but rather the precharged two- to five-gallon tanks available from Sears or plumbing suppliers. The T-12 by 3-T's Products works well.

Using a hand-held sink water sprayer at the toilet instead of an automatic refill will save water and frequency of emptying the holding tank. The sprayer allows wetting the bowl and pressure rinsing, while using less water and electricity. (This method is not recommended for recirculating toilets.)

FIGURE 4.3: The T-12 Constant-Flow Water Pressure Equalizer. (Courtesy 3-T's Products)

* * *

Before we move on to RV heating, cooling and refrigeration, perhaps another word on load management is in order. Use lights and appliances only when needed, and turn them off when leaving the RV. On cloudy days, when solar panels generate less than full output, limit your appliance use. In any event, use your regulator/ meter to gauge battery capacity, and take the time to understand your solar system.

RV SPACE HEATING

The typical RV furnace is an abysmal creation that will use all your propane in a weekend and kill your battery overnight. It's easy to say, "If you need lots of heat, you should move." But many people like winter sports, and accident or illness can strand you in a very cold area. A forced-air furnace *may* be desirable if your RV is used in such a climate or if hook-ups are a regular event. Almost all serious RVers now use catalytic heaters—very low propane consumers that require no electricity. Figure 4.4 shows a catalytic heater, and Table 4.1 compares it to a forced-air furnace to help you make your selection.

In the catalytic heater, a platinum-impregnated pad sets up a chemical reaction with oxygen and propane which releases energy at a temperature well below the flashpoint of many materials—a welcome safety feature. The heat is radiated, like sunshine, warming your body and the surfaces of nearby objects. Re-radiation warms the entire area.

Automatic vent fans are not necessary with most catalytic heaters. The circuit board will fail if a problem arises, and most rigs

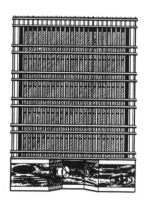

FIGURE 4.4: This compact catalytic heater is wall-mounted, requires no battery power, has a fully adjustable heat range, built-in piezoelectric spark lighter, and can be used at any elevation.

Table 4.1: RV Catalytic Heater vs Forced-Air Furnace

Catalytic Heater	Forced-Air Furnace
No battery power required.	Can draw battery down overnight. Uses up to 7 amps per hour.
Heats by radiation so no blower is necessary.	Blazing fire inside furnace. Produces carbon monoxide, which is vented outside with wasted heat energy.
Reduced fire hazard. Heats to only 425°F. No carbon monoxide produced.	
Reduced operating costs. Continuously uses only 3.6 oz of propane per hour.	Uses up to 2 gallons of propane per day. You pay for the heat exhausted outside, too.
Continuous gentle heat. Adjustable setting.	Hot blast of 25,000 BTU heater cycles on-and-off—all or nothing.
High-efficiency—nearly 100%. All heat remains inside.	Low efficiency. Loses almost as much heat outside as used to heat the RV's interior.

have adequate venting. One window just barely opened (24 square inches of fresh air) is all that's needed for safety, comfort, and condensation reduction.

Heaters with "oxygen depletion sensors" (ODS) are not recommended either. They are not necessary, can't be bypassed, and can fail just when heat is needed. Furthermore, ODS models may not work at elevations above 5000 feet.

RV COOLING

Various means of cooling are available to the RVer. Each has different advantages when it comes to effectiveness or energy conservation. It all depends on the weather.

RV Air Conditioning

Efficient battery-powered air conditioning is still in the future. There are no 12-volt refrigerated air conditioners. RV air conditioners operate from large generators. They will also operate from a large inverter, but the amp draw makes this method impractical. So, if you must have air conditioning, we recommend commercial power.

Evaporative Cooling

In arid climes, an evaporative cooler will do an excellent job. To be effective, a complete air change must occur every 1 to 3 minutes. Window or vent openings must equal at least 1 square foot for each 750 cubic feet per minute of air movement.

Relative humidity plays an important part in effective evaporative cooling. Table 4.2 compares the outside temperature with relative humidity to illustrate the cooling effect. Note that as humidity increases, the cooling effect decreases. Technically, evaporative cooling reaches its limit at 20° lower than the outside temperature. Proper ventilation and insulation are the keys to comfort.

Table 4.2: Outside Temperature Compared with Relative Humidity

Temperature Outside (°F)	Outside Relative Humidity							
	5%	10%	15%	20%	30%	40%	50%	60%
	Temperature Inside (°F)							
80	56	58	60	61	64	67	69	72
90	62	64	66	68	72	75	78	81
100	68	70	73	75	79	83	87	90
110	74	77	80	82	87	92	95	—
120	79	83	86	89	95	100	—	—

Several evaporative cooler models are available. They all consume too much electricity and water, but with simple modifications of blade pitch and water delivery the efficiency can be improved. Water consumption equals one-half gallon per hour minimum. But at least when it's hot, there is usually lots of sun on the solar panels! For solar applications, a high-quality evaporative cooler is a good substitute for air conditioning. Two solar panels and two batteries afford 8 to 10 hours of cooling per day in addition to your basic minimum lighting needs.

Power Ventilators

Power ventilators mount in the roof openings and provide three speeds of ventilation as well as an exhaust capability. They afford natural cooling, without the use of water, and are especially effective at night and in shady locations. Evaporative cooling can be achieved by hanging wet towels over windows and turning the power vent to exhaust to cool the incoming air.

Roof vent fans with thermostats can provide breeze-like air movement and prevent stagnant hot air build-up. The turbine-type, 12-inch diameter Fan-Tastic (Figure 4.5) will mount in a standard vent hole, and its three-speed motor will move from 577 to 942 cubic feet of air per minute. More amps are required for this unit than for the smaller fans usually placed in standard vents, but the thermostat controls help maintain an even, comfortable temperature.

FIGURE 4.5: A rotary blade vent fan. (Courtesy Fan-Tastic Vent Corporation)

RV REFRIGERATION

Standard RV refrigerators, primarily propane, have served us well for many years. They are constantly being improved and are used by many fixed-home owners as well—particularly solar-electric homeowners. If the RV is your home away from home, a refrigerator is essential. Size selection is a personal matter. Most RVs come from the factory with a box that has less than 7.3 cubic feet of interior space. Replacements up to 17 cubic feet are available, but remember that the larger the area of cooling, the more power consumed.

Other selection criteria include cost, efficiency, and energy source—propane or 12VDC. Seeking 120VAC hook-ups defeats the freedom of self-containment, and the power requirements rival those of air conditioning or electric heating for pure inefficiency. A standard 120VAC refrigerator uses 2 to 4 or more kWh of 120VAC power each day. This is equivalent to the energy supplied, in one day, by more than 16 solar panels under ideal conditions. In America, refrigerators alone account for 7% of the total electric energy produced, or 20% of your home electric bill.

It is impossible to predict the exact energy efficiency of even the best refrigerator because personal use patterns vary wide. Power consumption is affected by the ambient temperature of the room, frequency of inserting warm foods, habitual opening of the door, and length of time the door remains open.

The efficiency of any refrigerator can be increased by adding extra insulation to the top, sides, and door. Preventing or removing heat build-up in the compartment behind a propane refrigerator will greatly improve performance. Add awnings and park so that the refrigerator wall is away from the sun.

Improve ventilation and circulation around heat-producing components. A low-consumption circulating fan draws cool air up and over the condenser coils. Nicro solar fridge fans offer an effective and inexpensive unit that is solar-operated. Refrigerator fans work best if placed to draw air *past* the coils rather than at them. Do not place a fan close to the roof vent: the air flow will be reflected back into the unit and will create more problems that it solves. As with so many RV tips, common sense is essential.

Propane and super-insulated refrigerator are available options for RVers. Propane refrigerators are quite efficient. They use only 1 to 2 gallons of propane per week, are self-contained, and use little electricity. Some disadvantages are the inconvenience of locating and handling reserves of propane, small size, poor insulation, and the need for leveling. And a new generation of super-insulated refrigerators with low-voltage compressor units has emerged. These models use only 20% of the power AC home models use and can be powered by solar panels. (Note that these are *not* the currently popular automatic RV refrigerators, but something else entirely. Those models are discussed below.)

Low-Voltage Refrigerators

The 12-volt refrigerator/freezer models now available require little maintenance and the placement of the heat-generating compressor and condenser on top rather than beneath the cold storage area has improved efficiency. Chest-type designs save even more energy by keeping the cold air in the box when the door is opened. This design is reminiscent of early AC refrigerators with their thickly insulated walls. In those models, the motor was located above the box to disperse heat, in contrast to today's self-defeating models in which the motor is placed beneath the thinly insulated compartment it is trying to cool—all for the sake of good looks and compactness.

Another feature of the new compressor units is that they work satisfactorily while being "off-level" up to 30°. A gas model requires leveling if off-level 3° or more.

We have reviewed several of the high-efficiency refrigerator/ freezers, and a comparison of their size, power, and efficiency follows. Some are not as compatible to 100% solar as you might expect. Examine running duty cycle and amp draw carefully before selecting a 12VDC refrigerator/freezer.

The Sun Frost refrigerator/freezer, very popular with home-owners, is attractive to RVers because of the innovations which achieve exceptionally low power consumption. The Sun Frost (Figure 4.6) is super-insulated with 3 to 4 inches of polyurethane foam. A top-mounted, hermetically sealed compressor runs cool

FIGURE 4.6: The Sun Frost refrigerator/freezer. (Courtesy Sun Frost)

and prevents heat from entering the cabinet. A high level of efficiency is developed in a "low differential" evaporator coil.

Sun Frost models range from 4 to 17 cubic feet. The larger model (24VDC) contains a 3.5 cubic foot freezer between the upper and lower refrigerator sections, where it is buffered from thermal change. This model requires two compressors, though, whereas the smaller model uses just one. The freezer section will maintain 10°F and may be set for 0°F, but with an accompanying increase in power consumption.

Sun Frost models were designed for home use. Although RV-ready, some remodeling is necessary: reworking the cabinets and improvising retainers to replace glass shelves. Condensation is so minimal in this refrigerator that crispers and closed compartments are unnecessary, and its super-insulation allows 24-hour shut-off without spoilage.

We chose a 10 cubic foot Sun Frost and overall are very pleased. Its single compressor runs on about 5.75 amps for approximately 20 minutes per hour. Based on our usage patterns and ambient room temperature over a six-month period including cold and hot weather, our average amp draw is quite good: 40 AH per day. Technically, this unit could run on the output of only two standard panels; however, this would not allow any reserve for bad weather. We allow three panels full output just for refrigeration.

Some full-time solar users require up to four panels under ideal sunlight conditions, with at least one to four batteries dedicated to refrigeration. Eight panels and eight batteries could be required in locations with prolonged inclement weather.

Norcold manufactures a wide selection of quality 120VAC or 12VDC units ranging from a 3 cubic foot chest to a 7 cubic foot upright. Thin-wall insulation and placement of the compressor beneath the unit are drawbacks. Current draw is 8 amps—daily average of 5 amps at 120 AH per day. Compare this with the 40 to 48 AH per day rating of the high-efficiency unit described above.

Birken Manufacturing Company offers several box styles in 4 to 6 cubic foot sizes under the name Arctic Kold. The Arctic Kold compressor operates as efficiently as the Sun Frost. However, in the Arctic Kold model manufactured to "fit" in existing RV space, insulation is quite skimpy and overall amp draw rises accordingly.

Marvel Division produces compact refrigerator/freezers with excellent finishes and smooth ABS plastic liners. These rugged units are used by marine and remote biomedical labs for critical storage. A fan is mounted under the main compartment with the compressor. A special chest-type has a eutectic-salt storage area.

Build Your Own

Building a super-insulated refrigerator/freezer is not that difficult. Using one of the precharged compressor/condenser packages listed below, you can design a 7 to 10 cubic foot model which would rival a more expensive unit. Kits contain electronic controls, compressor, precharged tubes, and evaporator assembly for use in your specially designed "box." The Danfoss DC compressor is a long-standing favorite among efficiency experts because of its high reliability.

The Cold Machine by Adler-Barbour features the Danfoss compressor and 15-foot precharged tubes. This unit has been used for years on sailboats since the system can be fitted to widely varying hull shapes. Draw is 5.4 amps.

The Ice Device by Marvel is similar in design to the Cold Machine. Its American-made quality is unequaled for reliability. This conversion kit for remote location units offers a size range up to 15 cubic feet and features low-volt cutoff. Draw is 5.5 amps.

Arctic Kold by Birken Manufacturing incorporates an external brush-type motor to drive a sealed compressor. It is not a hermetic-type unit, and brush replacement is necessary. The kit is offered for box sizes up to 10 cubic feet. It includes 15-foot precharged lines and draws 5.75 amps. A horizontal or vertical evaporator box is available.

Norcolder by Norcold offers a single 40-watt or double 80-watt compressor for converting or homebuilding units up to 12 cubic feet: 12 feet of precharged lines attach to a unique flat or corner L-shaped evaporator. Amp draw is 4.5 per compressor.

Note: Do not confuse the above units with solid-state thermoelectric units like the Koolatron. These are good coolers, but are best used only while driving. Thermoelectric units use *many* amps by displacing small amounts of heat at low efficiency. If you have lots of amps to spare, these units could use them all while providing cooling—not freezing—for only one to two cubic feet.

Absorption Refrigeration

Absorption refrigerator/freezers are durable, have no moving parts, and should have a long reliable life, if used properly. Understanding the operation of an absorption unit may save you expensive repairs.

Using propane or electricity as a heat source, absorption units operate on a principle similar to that of a coffee percolator. The refrigerant solution—ammonia, water, and hydrogen—is heated to 325°F in the boiler tube causing percolation to the rectifier assembly where condenser fins remove the heat. The solution passes into the refrigerator where condensation and evaporation of the vapors create temperatures as low as −20°F in the low-temperature evaporator—and thus causes the cooling effect in the "cold plate" (see Figure 4.7). The spent solution then returns by gravity to the boiler, and the process is repeated.

FIGURE 4.7: Sibir's absorption unit does not require any 12-volt power in the propane mode. Note the evaporator coil and cold plate, and the fully adjustable freezer and refrigerator shelves.

Although 6° off-level is allowed front-to-back, an absorption unit must be level from side-to-side within 3° to prevent vapor lock caused by pooling of the refrigerant solution. Some of the salts in solution can crystallize and block portions of the tubing. The process is additive, and repeated operation off-level, for even short periods, can lead to total compaction. This problem can be avoided by periodically turning the unit off, leveling, and re-lighting.

Adequate ventilation of the condenser fins is necessary for proper cooling. During hot weather, you might find it difficult to keep ice frozen because of the differential temperature with outside air. Use a vent fan on the outside condenser coils, place an awning on the RV's outside wall, and park in a shaded area. Some safety precautions are also in order. Check roof vents and clear any obstruction—a bird's nest can be a fire hazard. Monitor your propane regulator for proper setting. Check for blocked or corroded boiler pipe, and for pilot light blowout while on the road.

In the 1920s, Electrolux manufactured absorption refrigerators that were used widely in Sweden and marketed in America under the name Servel. A similar design is available today from Dometic, Norcold, Sabir, and Sanyo. If you are tied to 120VAC, electric-absorption refrigerators are economical and hard-working. Some operate on 12VDC, but in this mode none are efficient. The attractive price of one currently advertised electric-absorption model might lead you to believe it has low power requirements. But away from a hook-up, unless you are driving continuously, your charging system will not be able to keep up with the power consumed.

Automatic Energy-Selecting (AES) Models

The new AES refrigerators available from Dometic, Norcold, and others automatically switch from one heat source to another if one source fails or is turned off. A built-in 12-volt heating element draws lots of amps. Whether you are switched to 120VAC, an AC generator or propane, the system still relies on a continuous supply of 12VDC to run the electronic brain, solenoid valves, and the electronic igniter where about 170 MA is required from the battery.

The 12VDC option can be used only while driving, but the average 23-amp draw translates into 553 AH per day. If your auxiliary battery is run down, even after a day of driving, perhaps your alternator just can't meet refrigeration needs, automotive requirements, and auxiliary battery recharge.

Your AES refrigerator will not work if your battery is run down or removed. Use an isolator (see chapter 3) so as not to discharge your starting battery should a malfunction occur or should you forget to turn off the ignition. Some self-sufficient folks reinstate "self- control" to these units by placing switches in the ignition wire and 120VAC line. A 12-volt drain remains, however—about 2 to 3 AH per day.

Small chest-type units are very effective freezers for RVers who use propane only.

Back to Propane

Use the refrigerator which offers the most efficiency for the purpose intended. The new high-efficiency models may be expensive, but return the investment in energy bill savings when using conventional sources. A super-insulated solar-powered refrigerator assures independence, but the cost of the unit plus the extra solar panels and battery capacity required might not be within your budget. Propane-fueled absorption refrigerators work very well, remain the most cost-efficient option available, and are quite compatible with the independence afforded through solar battery charging for all other electrical requirements.

5

THE RV SOLAR SYSTEM

The solar electric system and the RV are natural partners. RV power requirements for basic comforts are comparatively small, and the RV already has a ready-made low-voltage system. Lights, TV/radio, air circulation, water pump, and small appliances can all be easily accommodated by a solar battery charging system. Because light values differ from day to day, season to season, and place to place, the degree of charge will vary. Nonetheless a solar system will work slowly and silently to maintain your battery at 100% full charge.

Conservation is the secret to balanced, economical RV power with any electrical system. Good conservation practices and sufficient battery capacity can carry your solar system through the worst possible weather. The RV alternator is a ready back-up charging source, but if you are not willing to cut back and compromise a bit with the weather, you may choose to use a back-up generator. A moderately sized solar system, in combination with the RV's alternator (and generator, if you so choose), is the most versatile and least expensive way to go. The self-sufficiency and quantity of electricity demanded will determine the best proportions for system design.

A solar-equipped RV is the choice for those who seek energy independence. With a few simple modifications and a basic solar equipment package, the production RV can become a self-sufficient, go-anywhere power company. We've discussed solar panel operation and output characteristics, and batteries. Now we will describe the solar system itself.

PANEL SELECTION

Today's commercially manufactured solar panels produce a usable amount of power even under light conditions as low as 5% full sun. At noon on a clear day, the sun is said to be "one sun intensity," 100 milli-watts per square centimeter—full sun—to which all other light conditions are proportional. Solar panels are rated by the number of watts they can produce at peak power at full sun, and the high-efficiency types produce about 10 + watts per square foot of panel.

A solar panel's efficiency, and rating, are affected by the technical considerations we described earlier: namely, the number and size of cells in series, light intensity, and ambient temperature. Two other factors that affect output efficiency—orientation to the sun and the effects of permanent shading or intermittent shadows—will be addressed in the mounting and installation sections. The only other factor that comes to mind is the accumulation of dust and dirt on the panel. Just clean the panels off regularly with a soft cloth and glass cleaner.

Solar panels are extremely sturdy and when handled properly will last indefinitely. Within the panel, series of solar cells are sandwiched between layers of clear vinyl and silicone sealer. The connectors between cells are made redundant for added reliability. A special tempered glass front surface protects against the elements and can withstand the impact of heavy hail stones. It also promotes transmission of a higher percentage of light energy than conven-

FIGURE 5.1: Solar panel mounting. Note wire over the edge of the RV which allows side wall entry.

tional glass. The back surface is hermetically sealed with a specially coated and encased metal foil, and a sturdy full-perimeter, corrosion-resistant aluminum frame offers a place for mounting structure attachments.

Costs

The cost of a solar system for an RV is comparable to that of a generator—a real bargain when considering the benefits that solar affords. The power output of one or two panels may seem small, but keep in mind that not only is no fuel required, but the *total* power generated day after day is substantial compared to other charging methods. In fact, the cost for a specified amount of solar battery charging amortized over just a year or two is actually lower than the fuel costs alone of a generator. Add in park fees and maintenance or replacement costs of conventional systems, and the financial advantages of solar become even more obvious.

Future technological developments may bring costs down somewhat, though not appreciably within the next five years. Rumors of breakthroughs in mass manufacture abound, but rarely do they become reality in regard to price. For RV applications, certainly, solar is cost-effective today.

Numerous solar panels are available that differ in output voltage, amp rating—and price. Selection can be confusing, so shop around before you buy. Most importantly, you want a solar panel that will meet your energy requirements and bears the rated output capacity that you have decided is correct for you.

Prices of solar panels can range from $100 for a 10-watt trickle charger to $900 for 100 watts, or about $9 per watt. Remember, watts are a general measure of power derived by multiplying load amps and load volts. While cost per watt is a consideration, if you base your decision on price per watt alone you may end up with a panel that looks good and fits your available space, but that doesn't have the power you need.

A solar panel for a 12-volt RV system must be able to supply 15 to 16 volts of charge *under load*—thus a panel of 32 to 36 solar cells. Aside from correct voltage, the real measure of a solar panel at work is "peak amps" output. Only when you take these factors into account can you make a true comparison of dollars per watt. You get the best deal when you look for maximum amps at a correct design voltage.

Once you have decided on solar, done some homework and sized your system, the next hurdle is to find a source. Whereas it is best to purchase batteries locally, that might not be possible with the panels. First, many retail energy stores are not oriented toward the RV market and so their prices may be beyond your means. If you don't have access to an RV solar supplier, you might choose mail-order and the do-it-yourself method: components or a pre-packaged system. Or you might order through your local RV store and have the system installed for you. Be cautious about "bare bones" systems. Insist on a good warranty on power output, a regulator that operates automatically even when the RV is idle, meters that are easy to read and that accurately indicate battery state-of-charge (not color-coded zone meters), and a tiltable solar panel mount if you plan wintertime use.

Solar charging systems are of modular design and can be easily expanded. Be sure to verify this feature. Also keep in mind that you can mix solar panels from different manufacturers to meet future needs in your own system as long as the panels have the same design voltage.

REGULATION OF THE SOLAR CHARGING SYSTEM

The regulation or control of charging is a vital component of any battery system—automotive alternator, generator or solar. A regulator's primary purpose is to protect the battery from overcharge. Many unpredictable variables can put the automotive RV system at risk of overcharge, and with a solar system the seasonal temperature changes in themselves warrant use of a regulator.

During sunny periods panels produce more power than can be consumed and batteries may consequently be filled by early morning. Without regulation an overcharge state will be reached by noon and can result in gassing, excessive loss of electrolyte, and possible internal damage to the battery. A regulator allows your electrical requirements to vary while maintaining protection to the battery. It operates automatically, offers diode protection, and often includes meters for system monitoring.

There are self-regulating panels available that are excellent in certain direct applications like pump operation, but lack sufficient voltage to provide adequate charging for a fully operational RV's batteries, especially during warm weather, because they only contain 30 solar cells. They are cheaper and generally can't overcharge a battery (self-regulating) by virtue of the fact that they contain only two or three fewer solar cells than the panels we have been discussing. Further, because there is no regulator or diode, it is possible to boil a battery dry when the system is not in use. Keep in mind that any solar panel can be self-regulating—it is a matter of carefully balancing three factors: power produced, power consumed, and storage capacity of the battery bank.

A solar system that is sized to function properly for year-round use will produce a lot more power in summer than in winter. Sufficient battery capacity for this extra power will ensure available reserves for cloudy days, the ideal match being one battery per solar panel. Just as a trickle charger of less than one amp is not able to overcharge a battery, larger systems can function safely without a regulator if battery capacity is sized to exceed solar charging capacity. If solar peak output is less than 1 to 2% of the AH rating of the battery, for example, a 50-watt (3-amp) panel connected to three RV batteries, a regulator is not essential. But as this is not the norm, the average RV system should have the protection of a regulator.

Self-regulation by means of a manual switch to turn the panel power off or on requires the use of a hydrometer plus constant monitoring with a voltmeter. It is possible to balance production against storage and consumption in this manner if you exercise care in your measuring and monitoring and if you always remember when to re-activate or de-activate your system.

A solar (PV) regulator keeps battery voltage within acceptable levels and renders the solar system completely automatic. It is not designed for use with other charging systems, just as automotive-type regulators with current-consuming solenoids and relays are not to be used with solar panels. PV regulators come in two basic types: relay and solid-state. Their convenience and the battery protection they afford make them well worth the minimal expense involved.

In a relay regulator, the control circuit tells the relay when to open as the charge reaches full. It closes when the sun begins to shine on the panel. This type of regulator can also be used to divert or switch loads off when the battery indicates low or full, as needs be.

Whereas relay regulators have mechanical contacts which will wear with time, solid-state modules have no moving parts and ensure a long, reliable life. A transistor switches the solar panel power on and off as the control circuits indicate. No external diodes are required to prevent feedback of current at night.

There are many solid-state regulators on the market, some quite expensive. Most just prevent overcharge. Some have combination meters that are invaluable in determining the amount of power you have to "spend." Aside from visual monitoring and voltage while charging is stopped, ampere checks on the panel power, and overload protection, some sophisticated set-ups in-

FIGURE 5.2: The POWER GUARD™ regulator and monitor. (Courtesy RV Solar Electric)

clude temperature compensation, generator start-up, digital readout, load disconnect, and warning signals.

RV Solar Electric has designed a compact solid-state regulator with integrated meters specifically for RV use. The POWER GUARD automatically monitors, controls charge, and protects by cutting the charge rate back when it senses that the batteries are full and allows adjustments of setpoints for level of fill by the owner. Its observable functions—by expanded scale voltmeter— show how much stored power remains in the battery at any given time as well as the amps rate of recharge to the battery. It contains an adjustable outlet for trickle-charging the starting battery on motorhomes.

MOUNTING AND ORIENTATION

Mounting and positioning solar panels for maximum efficiency in an RV system is different than for a residence. But the objective is the same: to expose the panels to sunlight for as long as possible each day, especially during the peak hours of 10 am to 2 pm. Whereas a homeowner simply mounts a panel on the roof and points it in the right direction, an RV and its roof are constantly changing position. Because an RV can be parked anywhere, in any

FIGURE 5.3: Panels mounted side by side. The hardwood mounting pads increase support on a roof with thin sheet metal.

FIGURE 5.4: For difficult rafter spacing, one solution is mount the panels on a "cross roof" aluminum brace.

FIGURE 5.5: These solar panels are mounted within the framework, which conceals the panels when viewed from the side or below.

FIGURE 5.6: Custom-designed RV topped with four completely concealed solar panels.

position, aiming is not a one-time decision. Actually, this mobility can be used to great advantage: Just park the RV to get the best sun.

To do this, you need to keep the roof in mind when parking. All-day parking in total, or even partial, shade can reduce daily power to a trickle. Trees and buildings can create long shadows, and the shade of TV antennas or roof air conditioners will also reduce power output. Shading can cause severe reduction of power on short winter days, and during the heat of summer when it is natural to seek a cooler (shaded) site. Proper parking, however, can offset power loss. In summer, position the RV to receive morning shade, open sky overhead for a few hours, and shade again in the hot afternoon. Just three to four hours—between 10 am and 2

FIGURE 5.7:
An extra-compact layout of three panels allows them to be snuggled within the luggage rack on this van. Note invisible side view. Wind deflector hides the rear view.

FIGURE 5.8: A top view of the concealed panels mounted on the van in Figure 5.7.

pm—of peak summer sun is usually sufficient to keep your battery charged.

Some RVers prefer to separate the solar panel mounting completely from the roof because they have multiple uses for their system. A quick disconnect feature will facilitate RV and home use. While shading can be effectively eliminated with these portable panel mounts, there are other problems to consider. First, such portability increases the possibility of theft. Second, because panels are not bolted to a secure structure, caution must be exercised to protect them from breakage due to wind, vehicles, or passersby. It is better to use a heavy tripod or sawhorse than to place the panel against the coach or a nearby rock. Furthermore, the physical handling this mounting scheme requires increases the likelihood of accidental breakage, and so is not desirable to many RVers

Actual mounting instructions will be given in chapter 6. Basically, panel mountings for the RV should be simple and strong enough to withstand the wind pressure of highway driving. Securely attaching panels to the RV roof is the most troublefree method. Most manufactured frames come in one-panel and dual-panel sizes for easy arrangement on the roof. Single-panel mounts are convenient alongside vents or roof air conditioners. Mounting structures should offer an easy option for panel tilting.

Tilting and Orientation Adjustments

During summer, solar panels are best left in the flat, or travel, position because the sun is directly overhead. But in winter, when the sun is low in the southern sky, aiming the panels accordingly will increase power production. If your system is sized for summer loads, you may need to tilt your panels for winter use. Good mounting structures offer two-directional tilting with the removal of just one bolt on each end. Tilt the panels only if you plan to be parked for a week or more in one spot. The farther north (e.g., Canada), the greater the tilt angle required, and the longer your panels should be left tilted. Tilting panels about 45° to the south during December, January, and February can increase output by up to 40%.

We have seen many examples of adjustable mounts ranging from clever turntable frames to sophisticated freon-powered sun-tracking systems. Some, while quite ingenious, are often complicated and expensive. Others are impractical or downright laughable. Most require frequent adjustment.

A simple solution to tilting, orientation, and tracking complexities is to add an extra panel to compensate for winter inefficiency. Tilt occasionally if required, and park your RV to maximize efficiency.

FIGURE 5.9: Note that in this solar panel mount holes in the mounting leg allow variation in tilt angle.

FIGURE 5.10: The best efficiency during wintertime is gained by tilting panels to 45° facing south. This is only practical if you will be parked in one location for two weeks or more.

FIGURE 5.11: This custom-made rotating and tiltable base offers maximum wintertime use. Panels are flat at all other times.

FIGURE 5.12: Panels tilted south for winter usage.

PREPACKAGED SYSTEMS

Simple and straightforward, today's prepackaged RV solar systems can be installed the day they are received, even by the "unhandy." Some RVers prefer to purchase and assemble components separately, but the convenience of obtaining everything you need in a single package can save time and money.

We had to research and select individual components for our original starter system because no prepackaged systems were available. To meet our own needs—and in response to the interest of many other RVers—we designed our own package at RV Solar Electric. Available in several sizes, the RV POWERPAC is a fully engineered solar charging system specially designed for RV hook-up, placement, and use. You supply the RV and battery capacity. The RV POWERPAC supplies virtually everything you need to achieve solar battery charging:

1. Siemens Solar Panels—with a 10-year warranty, approval by Underwriters Labs, and worldwide recognition as one of the highest-quality solar panels.

2. Regulator/Meters—the POWER GUARD (described earlier) for visual monitoring, evaluating, and regulating the solar system.
3. Wiring and Hardware—including UV, weather-resistant wire harness of color-coded #12 gauge, to make hook-up easy.
4. Mounting Structure—single- or dual-panel configuration designed with RV placement in mind.
5. Detailed Installation Instructions—step-by-step for the do-it-yourself RVer.

The RV POWERPAC is completely modular and can be easily expanded. The POWERPAC 1 is a one-panel starter system adequate for lights, TV, and water pump for the thrifty single RVer who stays parked for a limited time. Systems of three and four panels provide the extra margin of power needed for AC inverter systems or for long-term use in areas with unpredictable weather.

Our advice to those new to this technology is to start small and add on. Original equipment can remain intact, so the cost of adding solar capacity is only the cost of an additional solar panel and the corresponding battery. No added internal wiring is necessary, and only a minimal amount of time is required to expand a system. Even if you change RVs, solar electric systems are easy to move from one to another. Removing the equipment and wiring, sealing a few holes, and re-installing on your new rig should take only a few hours.

Whatever components or prepackaged systems you choose, insist on an RV-specific instruction manual and hold on to it. Whether you do-it-yourself or have someone else install the system, illustrations of what goes where and how it works will enable you to use the system to full advantage.

SIZING THE RV SOLAR SYSTEM

Sizing an RV solar system requires a little homework, but the procedure is quite straightforward:

1. Determine your daily power consumption.
2. Determine the number of solar panels needed to meet your consumption requirement.
3. Determine the battery storage capacity needed to match your solar system's production and consumption.

In this section we will discuss each step and provide worksheets and real-life system examples to aid you in the sizing process—whether you are interested in a combination system or one that is 100% solar. Remember that the charging sources you already have can be used in conjunction with your system. Your alternator charges while driving, and that generator powers 120VAC appliances while charging also. Once your battery is full, it's up to you how to use it. Your conservation practices will determine how long the power supply will last.

Determine Your Power Consumption

To determine your daily "electrical budget," make a list of all the equipment you use in your RV—lights, TV, appliances—everything that draws current. Next, determine how long, in hours and fractions thereof, each item is used per day. The following Appliance Consumption Worksheet (Figure 5.13) lists the average amp draw for equipment commonly used in the RV. If an appliance you use is not on the list, check the appliance itself or its manual. Amp draw is usually listed for any electrical appliance; if not, it can be ascertained with an ammeter. We have averaged some common items in the list below.

Multiply the amp draw of each item by the length of time you use it to derive the total daily AH usage for each load. Add the totals to calculate your daily electrical consumption in AH.

If a one-panel system producing 20 AH per day was used to meet the modest requirements of this example, about 25% of the system's charging output could be stored in the battery or used for other purposes, like occasional vacuum cleaning or the substitution of a 3-amp color TV. Don't forget that additional electricity is produced through the vehicle's engine. In our example, we de-

Figure 5.13: Appliance Consumption Worksheet

Appliance	Approx. Current (amps @ 12 volts)	hrs/day	amp hours consumed
Lights			
incandescent			
1 bulb (25 watt)	2	x _____	= _____
1 bulb (50 watt)	4	x _____	= _____
quartz halogen			
(25 watt)	2	x _____	=
fluorescent			
1 tube (15 watt)	1	x _____	= _____
2 tubes (30 watt)	1.6	x _____	= _____
Entertainment			
9-in. color TV	3	x _____	= _____
12-in. B&W TV	1.1	x _____	= _____
CB receiver	0.5	x _____	= _____
stereo am/fm	1	x _____	= _____
equalizer/amplifier	2	x _____	= _____
satellite receiver	2	x _____	= _____
Cooling/Heating			
500 cfm fan	1.2	x _____	= _____
750 cfm fan	2.5	x _____	= _____
1000 cfm fan	5	x _____	= _____
forced-air furnace	5–8	x _____	= _____
evap. cooler (1200 cfm)	8	x _____	= _____
vent & range hood fan	2	x _____	= _____
RV water pump	8	x _____	= _____
DC compressor refrig.	6	x _____	= _____
3-way frig. on 12 V	35	x _____	= _____
_____	_____	x _____	= _____
_____	_____	x _____	= _____
_____	_____	x _____	= _____

The AC appliances listed below require the use of an inverter. The AC amps have been multiplied by 10 to show the DC amp draw from the battery. For example, 5 amp AC = 50 amp at 12VDC.

Appliance	Current	hrs/day	amp hours
Saber saw	50	x _____	= _____
Microwave oven	125	x _____	= _____
Blender	15	x _____	= _____
Slide projector	50	x _____	= _____
Electric typewriter	8	x _____	= _____
Computer	4	x _____	= _____
14-in. color TV	7	x _____	= _____
Sewing machine	10	x _____	= _____
Hair clippers	4	x _____	= _____
B/l vacuum	100	x _____	= _____
Electric broom	60	x _____	= _____
	Total amp hours used per day	=	_____

Table 5.1: An Example of a One-Panel System

Appliance	Approx. Amps	x	Avg hr/day	=	AH/day
15-watt fluorescent	1.0	x	6.0	=	6.0
12-volt incandescent	1.5	x	2.0	=	3.0
TV (9-in. B&W)	0.9	x	4.0	=	3.6
Water pump					
(PAR or Shurflo)	8.0	x	0.2	=	1.6
12-volt stereo	0.8	x	2.0	=	1.6
			Total AH Used in One Day		15.8

liberately omitted electric appliances that produce heat because of their excessive power requirements. Our intent here is to provide a reference point. When you compare it to the actual RV solar systems described later in the chapter, you will be better able to determine your own energy consumption—and to determine how conservative or extravagant you can be. Adjustments can always be made to balance preference, convenience, and basic necessities.

How Many Solar Panels?

The popularity of RVing may be partially attributed to its capacity to adapt to many lifestyles—obvious by the wide variety of RVs we see on the road. Consequently, the solar system you select will be determined to a great extent by your RV lifestyle. If you drive every other day and enjoy RV campgrounds with hook-ups, you probably have no interest in a 100% solar system. Perhaps you want a small trickle charger to maintain your battery while in storage. If you use your vehicle alternator to charge while driving and want the option of three to four days camping without hook-ups, a small solar system will accommodate you. If energy independence is your priority, and you want to spend an entire season in a remote spot without driving, solar can accommodate you, too.

Solar panels generate a predictable amount of power each day depending on where you are and the season. Most full-time RVers "follow the sun" and so automatically provide the ideal environment for solar battery charging. RVers who are not "sun worshippers" or "snow birds" need to gauge seasonal and climate variations when sizing their system. A solar system may be less productive in winter depending on the location.

Whereas conversion efficiency of a solar panel is increased with cooler temperatures, the amount of light available decreases in northern latitudes and in winter (Table 5.2). Correspondingly, winter power needs for lighting, TV, furnace, and so on, may be higher. Therefore a solar system sized strictly on summer needs might require a back-up charging source in winter; a system sized for 100% winter needs will overproduce in summer and so can power extra fans or a cooler.

Table 5.2: System Size Selection Chart

System Size (45- to 50-watt panels)	AH per (clear) day production	
	Winter	Summer
1-Panel System	15	24
2-Panel System	30	48
3-Panel System	45	72
4-Panel System	60	96

For efficiency and economy, we recommend that RVers compromise and size their solar systems to mid-year ratings and add panels later, if necessary or desired. The power available from sunlight has the same energy value when the sky is clear and bright, wherever you are. The objective is to expose the panels during the peak sunlight hours—generally between 10 am and 2 pm—to produce power for daily needs and reserve power for rainy or heavy overcast days. Tilting panels to increase production in winter, and recharging by occasional driving or the use of a back-up generator should meet the extra energy demands of December, January, and February. For many RVers, good conservation habits alone enable their systems (sized on mid-year ratings) to meet year-round needs.

Figure 5.14 shows the winter and summer power output and the rounded mid-year average of typical 3-amp solar panels, based on exposure to 8 hours of peak sunlight. Compare the AH figure that you calculated from the Appliance Consumption Worksheet. How many solar panels do you need to meet your energy needs?

For more hands-on information, actual system descriptions submitted by solar RVers follow the battery sizing section.

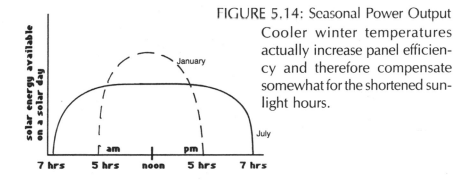

FIGURE 5.14: Seasonal Power Output Cooler winter temperatures actually increase panel efficiency and therefore compensate somewhat for the shortened sunlight hours.

BATTERY SIZING FOR YOUR SOLAR SYSTEM

Now that you have developed your electrical budget and have determined the number of solar panels you need to meet consumption, you are ready to match your system to its corresponding battery capacity.

Ampere hour capacity and deep-cycling capability are probably the most important considerations in selecting batteries for solar applications. The storage battery capacity needed is determined by the expected load and the longest period of time the system is expected to operate on batteries alone. Simply stated, the battery must have sufficient AH capacity to power a load until there is sufficient sunlight to recharge the battery.

For a small solar system, it is simple to oversize battery storage to ensure sufficient energy to operate the load. For large installations, where batteries can represent a considerable investment, a detailed assessment of load requirements will help contain your system to what is actually necessary.

FIGURE 5.15: Temporary panel placement, as on this camper van, offers battery charging capabilities. (Courtesy Nate Friend)

FIGURE 5.16. Less permanent battery placement can be located anywhere. (Courtesy Nate Friend)

FIGURE 5.17: Factory-design battery compartment for a large system—four 8-D batteries on a roll-out tray.

A typical RV battery set-up should provide at least six days storage capacity. To determine *minimum* battery capacity for a typical RV solar system, take the figure from the worksheet that you computed for daily AH consumed and multiply it by 6. For example:

15 AH daily consumption × 6 = 90 AH battery capacity

RV applications vary, of course. Space and weight constraints must be considered, as well as how long you individually will need battery reserves. If you plan to do much dry camping, it is advisable to double the minimum requirement given above, that is, multiply by 12 rather than 6. A general rule of thumb, developed from our experience, is:

1 solar panel + 1 (105 AH) battery per person

The capacity and condition of your present battery should be considered, as it can be put to good use in your solar electric system. The RVer's goal is to store the maximum amount of electricity in the smallest possible space. When you add batteries, recall the recommendations of chapter 3: deep-cycle design, group 27 RV/marine size, high charge rate with low gassing, and life rating over 200 cycles at 50% discharge. Series-connected 6-volt golfcart batteries and the new sealed, maintenance-free 12-volt model described in chapter 3 are also good choices. Battery freshness (check the manufacture date on the battery) and weight make local purchase preferable. Nationwide warranty coverage offers security.

SOLAR SYSTEM SIZING
Some Actual Examples

Sizing a solar system is best illustrated by real-life situations. So you can compare your usage patterns with those of others, we have gathered information from RVers who meet their energy needs with solar. Examples range from a 10-watt trickle charger to a four-panel system to 24-volt applications for the larger bus conversions or land yachts. Each example lists the owner's daily power consumption, the equipment used to supply it, and system costs.

Example 1: 5- to 10-Watt Trickle Charger

Charge Rate: 0.5 amp
Power Production:
3 to 5 AH per day
Cost: $10 per watt

A 5- to 10-watt trickle charger is of limited use as a power supply to a dry camper, but it is beneficial in maintaining starting/storage batteries that are not used for long periods of time. Use of a solar trickle charger with any 12-volt system—autos, trucks, aircraft, boats—will greatly extend battery life. The trickle charger can be permanently mounted on the RV roof, or it can remain portable for use anywhere. You can place the panel on the dashboard while traveling, or outside the windshield while stationary. Use the instant wiring capability of a cigarette lighter socket and plug adapter for charging. Check that your cigarette lighter is on when the ignition is off.

Example 2: One-Panel Solar System

Perry Stimson
18-foot mini-motorhome
Power Production:
15 to 24 AH per day

"I am a full-time RVer and belong to several membership parks. I spend winters in Arizona and Texas, dry camping usually less than five days before driving 100 miles or so between sites. In summer, I travel in New York to be near my family, and I use occasional hook-ups for air conditioning.

FIGURE 5.20: Single-panel mounting frame used where roof space is limited.

I am generally conservative in power consumption, but can be wasteful at times—especially in watching a lot of ball games on TV. I have never run short of power with my solar system, even when spending months at a time in the desert. In fact, in summer I produce more power than I can use."

Propane Appliances
Refrigerator, stove/oven, water heater, catalytic heater only

Electric Appliances and Daily Consumption

Appliances	hrs used	AH
incandescent bulb (1)	2	4
fluorescents (2 15-watt)	4	8
porch light (1)	1	2
blender (12-volt)	0.06	1
TV (9-in. B&W)	2	2
stereo	6	3
tire pump	occasional use	
vent fan	1	
water pump	1	
Total Consumed		22

Electric Equipment
60-amp automotive alternator (averages 30 amps while driving)
No back-up generator
2 group 27 size batteries (1 starting/1 deep-cycle)
One solar panel system (produces up to 24 AH/day) (Cost $500)

Example 3: Two-Panel Solar System
Charles and Lena House
27-foot Airstream trailer
Power Production:
30 to 48 AH per day

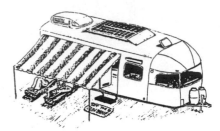

"We are part-time RVers, and prefer to dry camp. We spend 2 to 3 weeks in Mexico and California in winter, and the summers in Puget Sound, Washington. Though we park in the forest all summer, we have seldom run out of power (except when it rained for two weeks). We practice the conservative use of electricity."

Propane Appliances
Refrigerator, stove/oven, water heater, forced air furnace and catalytic heater

Appliances	hrs used	AH
incandescent bulbs (2)	3	12
fluorescents (1)	5	5
blender	0.03	3
TV (9-in. color)	2	6
stereo/CB		3
water pump		2
furnace	1	8
Total Consumed		39

Electric Equipment
Tow vehicle 45-amp auto alternator (unused when not hooked-up)
Two 105-AH deep-cycle batteries tongue-mounted
40-amp converter (unused when no utility connections)
500-watt portable generator (back-up generator seldom used)
Two 40-watt solar panels (produce up to 48 AH/day)
No inverter used (Cost $800)

Example 4: Two-Panel Motorhome Solar System
Noel and Barbara Kirkby and family
30-foot motorhome
Power Production: 30 to 48 AH per day

"Our family of five RVs part-time. In winter we camp locally (in Arizona) in seven-day intervals. During the summer, we go wherever we want, usually spending five days or less at any one location. Five people use lots of water so we have a large holding tank. Our use of energy is conservative for five people. We watch our meters daily. When we park in deep forest, we use the back-up generator/rapid charger as necessary."

Propane Appliances
Refrigerator, stove/oven, hot water, furnace and catalytic heater

Electric Appliances and Daily Consumption

Appliances	hrs used	AH
incandescent bulbs (3)	2	12
fluorescents (2)	3	6
TV (B&W)	6	6
stereo/CB	4	2
water pump		6
*B/l vacuum	0.15	12
*microwave	0.25	30
*chain saw		10
*blender	0.05	2
*hair curler	occasional use	
	Total Consumed	84

*AC appliances require the use of an inverter: DC to AC power.

Overuse of system varies. The 36-AH deficit comes from the battery reserves. The 525-AH battery pack affords us extended stays up to 14 days. One hour of rapid recharge through the inverter/charger gains back 75 AH (about equal to 1.5 days of solar recharge).

Electric Equipment
70-amp automotive alternator

Five 105-AH deep-cycle/marine batteries (525 AH total)
100-amp charger built-in inverter
2500-watt TRACE inverter/charger (cost $1300)
Two 50-watt solar panels (produce up to 48 AH per day) (Cost $900)

Example 5: Three-Panel Motorhome System

George and Liz Piveral
22-foot motorhome
Power Production:
45 to 75 AH per day

"We are full-time, 100% solar
RVers who winter in Arizona
and spend five months in Utah
each summer. We practice energy conservation and watch our
meters daily. Even so, we enjoy satellite TV and our Lowrey organ.
Living with your system day after day, you develop a feel for
conservation and when it is full you feel free to spend that energy
on any extra projects you need done. We watch special TV shows
with friends, and they are amazed at our power—generated without a noisy generator."

Propane Appliances
Refrigerator, stove/oven, water heater, gas light, catalytic heater

Electric Appliances and Daily Consumption

Appliances	hrs used	AH
incandescent bulbs (2)	2	8
fluorescents (2)	3	6
porch light	1	2
mixer	occasional use	
satellite TV	2	4
Lowrey organ	1	4
stereo	2	1
vent fan	0.5	1
water pump	0.5	5

vacuum	occasional use	
solder iron	occasional use	
*blender	0.05	2
*1/4-in. drill	0.2	1
	Total Consumed	34

*AC appliances require the use of an inverter: DC to AC power.

Example 6: Four-Panel Motorhome Solar System
Bill and Nancy Lance
32-foot luxury motorhome
Power Production:
60 to 100 AH per day

"We are full-time 100% solar RVers. We winter in Florida, Texas, California, and Arizona, and summer in Vermont, Michigan, Colorado, and at Yellowstone. We like to dry camp and tend to use electricity extravagantly. Overuse of the system occurs on busy days with good weather. We have used 6% more than replaced in battery, but made up for it on 'take it easy days.' Our batteries get us through overuse, so we don't worry since we check things out each week. That gives us peace of mind."

Propane Appliances
Refrigerator/freezer, stove/oven, water heater, furnace only

Electric Equipment
100-amp Lestek alternator
No built-in generator (use the extra storage space)
1200-watt Heart inverter—no charger option
400-AH+ batteries (one starting plus two 8-D truck batteries [208 AH ea])
4 solar panels (60 to 100 AH production) (Cost $1600)

Electric Appliances and Daily Consumption

Appliances	hrs used	AH
incandescent bulbs (4)	3	24
fluorescents (3)	4	12
halogen bulb (1 25-watt)	1.5	3
porch light	1	2
*kitchen tools		1
range fan	1	2
*microwave	0.9	4
*B/l vacuum	0.8	2.5
*TV (14-in. color)	2	9
stereo/CB	4	2
am/fm cassette		4
slide projector	0.25	13
*computer	3	5
*computer printer	0.5	3
*rock saw/polisher		6
*clippers	occasional use	
roof vent		2
evaporative cooler	occasional use	
furnace	occasional use	
water pump		4
ni-cad recharger		1
*1/4-in. drill	0.2	2
Total Consumed		106

*AC appliances require the use of an inverter: DC to AC power.

Large RVS, Bus Conversions, Land Yachts

Luxury motor coaches that weigh over 20,000 pounds are in a class all by themselves. Usually they are equipped with extra-heavy parts, lots of batteries (up to a half ton), 24-volt starting systems for big diesel engines, 12- or 15-kW power plants, and sometimes all-electric kitchens. This luxury fleet can also benefit from solar charging, though more as a supplemental than as a main power source. Here is how one large RV owner uses his system.

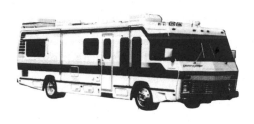

"When the 12-kW generator is used, a 150-amp rapid charger refills the 800 AH battery storage with almost a full charge. The four solar panels are great for filling the top 20% after the gen is turned off. They can then operate 'quietly' for hours. We use a lot of electric appliances through the 2500-watt inverter and 12-volt lights as well. Solar has saved us many hours of wear time on the generator, thus extending its life. The inverter provides instant 120VAC 24 hours a day. You can realize the value in this system especially after 'quiet hour.' We are enthusiastic about the multiple benefits we derive from the inverter/solar system"

Gene Martin
California

Large bus conversions, like remote homes, have higher power demands than the customary RV. Expanding the basic 12-volt system is easy. Use extra batteries, panels, and a back-up generator to make the system more durable. A 24-volt battery pack offers more efficiency for the larger system because it meets the heavier loads anticipated, such as shop tools, washing machines, refrigerators, and even well pumps. The 24-volt wires need to be only half as large as 12-volt systems for the same voltage drop.

Twelve volts to an inverter (see chapter 7) reaches a maximum output of 2500 when stepping from 12 to 120VAC. Efficiency within the electronics and battery supply are improved with 24VDC to 120VAC—a multiplier of only five times. The longer wire runs of a house have less voltage drop when operated at 24 volts.

Twelve-volt lights and appliances can also be operated from the 24-volt pack by "center tapping" or more effectively by using a battery equalizer. This device automatically draws from the 12-volt battery half with the highest available power, thus maintaining a balanced fail-safe system.

OTHER THAN RV SOLAR USES

Photovoltaic panels are used for many land-based and marine-type systems. Direct-connected water pumping replaces windmills. Remote homes far from the utility line and remote communication stations are workable alternatives. A home system has little regard for the extra weight and space required for batteries. Having plenty extra provides a buffer for bad weather or larger loads. Keep in mind that a home or marine system duplicates the RV system. The components are the same, but the number of panels, mounting method, appliances, and batteries may vary. *The New Solar Electric Home* by Joel Davidson (see Appendix B) is an excellent publication that will help you understand, design, install, and maintain a home system.

6

BASIC RV WIRING AND SOLAR SYSTEM INSTALLATION

RV WIRING

Wiring selection and installation can make the difference between an efficient system and one that is wasteful, problematic, and unsafe. Know where wires are located and the purposes for which they are intended. One of your first tasks is to draw a simple diagram of your system on graph paper. Next, place a tab on each wire and key those tabs to your diagram. Strips of peel-off lettered or numbered tabs are inexpensive and available from any electrical supplier (Figure 6.1).

```
←— PEEL BACK THIS ZIP-STRIP TO THE PIECE(S) YOU NEED
1  2  3  4  5  6  7  8  9  10 11 12 13 14 15 16 17 18 19 20 21 22 23 24 25 26 27
1  2  3  4  5  6  7  8  9  10 11 12 13 14 15 16 17 18 19 20 21 22 23 24 25 26 27
1  2  3  4  5  6  7  8  9  10 11 12 13 14 15 16 17 18 19 20 21 22 23 24 25 26 27
1  2  3  4  5  6  7  8  9  10 11 12 13 14 15 16 17 18 19 20 21 22 23 24 25 26 27
1  2  3  4  5  6  7  8  9  10 11 12 13 14 15 16 17 18 19 20 21 22 23 24 25 26 27
1  2  3  4  5  6  7  8  9  10 11 12 13 14 15 16 17 18 19 20 21 22 23 24 25 26 27
```

FIGURE 6.1: Diagram and label your system with adhesive wire markers like those shown here.

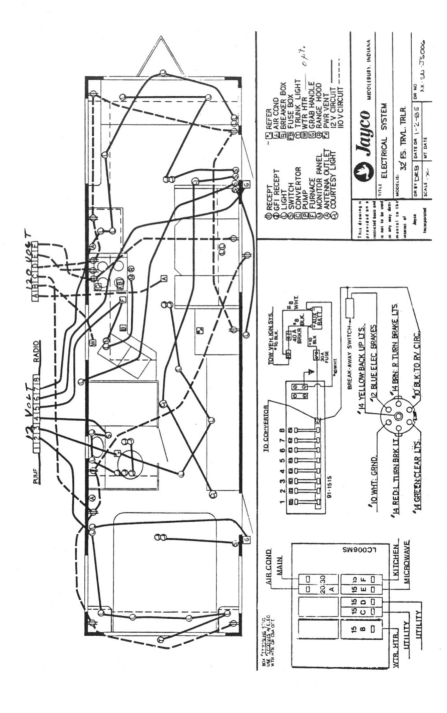

FIGURE 6.2: Jayco wiring layout showing 120VAC and 120VDC elements. (Courtesy of Jayco Inc.)

Keep in mind that you will be working with two wiring systems. Most RVs are dual-wired at the factory. The 120VAC system is usually reserved for the utility outlets and major equipment like air conditioning; separate outlets, direct-wired appliances, and built-in lighting circuits constitute the 12VDC system. (The principles are the same for 24VDC systems.) A typical wiring layout is shown in Figure 6.2.

Locating 120VAC elements from the standard circuit breaker load center is simple, but you may discover a potential safety hazard in that breakers are sometimes incorrectly labeled in manufacture. Operate them individually and check receptacles to find out what goes where. Note particularly the breaker that operates the converter—it should operate nothing else. If it does, you may have a spare breaker space which can be used, or you can "double-up" two of the lightly loaded utility outlet lines. Be careful—these are 120VAC lines. If you are going to fuss with them, turn off the power first.

Locating 12VDC lines and connectors can be more difficult, but at least you won't be electrocuted by low-voltage systems. Don't be casual, though—a short-circuit at the battery can cause a fire.

Most 12VDC lines will branch from a board at the converter. There may also be a fused board on the front of a trailer for tow-vehicle wiring. As solar panels, inverters, and other devices are added, there may be more junctions. At this point, the tendency is to stop diagramming, but in fact it's even more important to continue.

System Grounding

An RV is mounted on rubber tires and so system grounding differs from that of a structure with a foundation. In a 120VAC fixed residence, the white (neutral) wires are usually connected through a bonding screw that penetrates the connecting bar and contacts the box frame to the green (bare) ground wires. In a low-voltage fixed structure (e.g., a 12VDC remote cottage), a battery ground

(−) connection to a grounding rod or metal water pipe is recommended. However, because of the mobility and integral design of the RV, a ground rod connection is not necessary unless a 120VAC utility is attached. In the utility connection outside the RV, the neutral and bare wires usually run to earth ground. However, inside the RV breaker box, you will find two separate grounding bars—white (neutral) should go to the insulated bar, and green (bare) to the buss common to the box and battery ground (−) as well.

The RV battery negative (−) is attached to the chassis *and* coach skin, except in the rare positive (+) ground vehicle. Ground to chassis and skin also provides a beneficial capacitor effect for fluorescent lights, radios, TVs, and CBs by creating a shield and reducing reception interference.

Check Polarity

While you are looking at your breaker box, check for another hazard that can be created in manufacture. With the RV disconnected from park power, use a portable voltmeter to ensure that the "white bar" has not been connected to the box frame (ground). In the event it were connected to ground and you were to plug into a hook-up with reversed polarity (crossed wires) while touching the metal of the RV, *you* would become the path to ground. The entire metal frame of the RV would become the "hot" side of 120VAC.

These simple 120VAC "polarity checkers" are sold at any hardware store for about $5. Everyone should have one. Never plug an RV into a hook-up without checking its polarity. Also, use your portable voltmeter to determine polarity of all outlets and connections in your RV. Reverse polarity can damage or destroy fluorescent lights and stereo equipment. Check your generator for incorrect polarity, too. It's not uncommon to find a generator installed so that it can be plugged into the system at the same time the umbilical cord is plugged into a hook-up. The results can be disastrous!

Wire Type and Color Coding

Wire your electrical system with copper wire only. Two types of wire are available: *solid* (Romex cable, or individual wires used in homes and commercial buildings) and *multi-stranded* (commonly used in autos, boats, and RVs). Electrically, there is no difference between the current-carrying capacity of solid and stranded wire of the same gauge, but solid wire (Romex) is *not* recommended for RV use. It is difficult to route, vibration leads to breakage and loose connections, and crimp-on terminal connectors are possible only by soldering short lengths of stranded wire.

Multi-stranded wire is used in 12VDC RV and automotive wiring. It is flexible, easy to work in tight places, and accepts crimp-on terminal connectors. Automotive and electrical supply houses offer "auto primary" wire—the finer the inner strands, the more flexible the wire. Suggested wire types are auto primary wire designations THWN, THHN, THW, USE, and RHH; or Tray Cable (Type TC), a two-conductor, direct-burial cable which will not deteriorate when exposed to sunlight. Expensive and well worth it, TC is the type we use in our solar electric system.

Note that each DC receptacle, light, or appliance has two wires attached. Standard RV color coding is usually positive (+) *red* and negative (−) *black*. There is some variation among manufacturers and even among rigs. When black and white are used as a "pair," the standard code is black (+) and white (−). Again, label each wire end to avoid serious hazard. Reversing polarity—crossing the wires—can cause equipment malfunction, blown fuses, motor burn-out, and fire.

Wire Size and Voltage Drop

Properly sized wire is important for safety and efficiency. Wire size is designated by gauge number—the larger the wire, the smaller the gauge number. Main circuits are usually #10 gauge wire and serve several points from one circuit; #14 is the minimum size required for branch, or single-purpose, circuits. Wire that is too small in diameter uses up power through resistance, "burning off" valuable power as heat. Larger wire costs more but assures efficiency, safety, and less voltage drop.

The resistance which causes reduced voltage (drop) and slows the passage of current can be helpful. It allows us to reduce voltage and current deliberately when operating some very low voltage devices and when charging flashlight batteries. However, when unintentional, due to poor connections or too small a wire size, it can cause loss of power and equipment malfunction. (Keep in mind that some components, including a diode-containing regulator, automatically causes a 0.5-volt drop.)

If lights dim regularly when an appliance is turned on, check for poor connections first. If the connections are good, the wire size may be too small. You can install separate larger wires or run parallel wires of the same size from the source to the appliance. "Splitting up" circuits more evenly may also help reduce the load on any one circuit. Remember to provide equal wire "help" for the often forgotten negative line.

Use Table 6.1 to select the correct wire size. Select the next larger size (smaller gauge number) when sensitive electronics or inverters are used. Use twice the size indicated for hard-starting motor applications where 200% of running current is needed.

Table 6.1: Wire Gauge for 5% Voltage Drop
(12-volt Systems) (AWG)

Current (amps)	Wire Run to Load (feet)								
	10	15	20	25	30	35	40	45	50
4	14	14	14	14	14	14	14	14	12
6	14	14	14	12	12	12	10	10	10
8	14	14	12	10	10	10	8	8	8
12	12	12	10	10	8	8	8	6	8
15	10	10	10	8	8	8	6	6	6

Fuses Protect You and Your RV

Use a fuse or circuit breaker to prevent wires from becoming overheated—they can become red hot from a short circuit. A 35¢ fuse is well worth the peace of mind and fire protection it offers. When adding a new line to the system, always go through an existing branch circuit or add a new fuse as close to the power source (battery or converter) as possible. The idea is to protect the entire wire run.

Fuses do obstruct the flow of electricity to some small extent. Nevertheless, a very worthwhile technique is to install additional 5-amp, wired-in-line fuses at each lighting fixture. Troubleshooting a faulty circuit is much simpler when you have a blown fuse as the starting place. Should a problem arise, your diagram—listing each fuse location and its value—will save you time. Pick branch fuses sized 20 to 50% larger than the combined load of the circuit. A main fuse or circuit breaker for the whole 12VDC system is also helpful.

When several large batteries are hooked together and large #6 or #4/0 gauge wires supply heavy starters, the generator or inverter, a "catastrophe fuse" (located in the negative wire as it exits the battery) can avert a vehicle fire. An inexpensive, renewable construction fuse (Buss #REN300, 300-amp), available at any electrical supply house, can be bolted to the frame. A ground strap

FIGURE 6.3: Custom circuit breaker box replaces fuse panel. (Courtesy Country Camper)

FIGURE 6.4: A 350-amp catastrophe fuse for use in the negative wire at the vehicle frame.

is also advised. As ground, insulation is not critical, except to the negative post of the battery (see Figure 6.5).The 300-amp fuse is heavy enough to allow operation of the starter, inverter or generator, but will blow if a short-circuit occurs.

An ammeter in the discharge wire, between the batteries and the main fuse box, will show how much electricity is being used. Should an item be left "on," you will be alerted. A good "shunt type" ammeter with 20- or 30-amp scale will carry the load of heavy appliances and allow you to see small values. It is surprising how fast a few amps here and a few amps there add up.

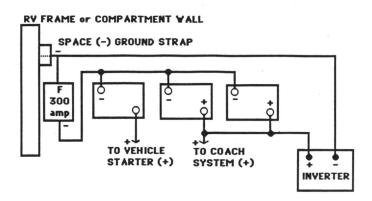

FIGURE 6.5: Adding a heavy-duty fuse in the negative line, rather than the positive line, prevents accidental short circuits or contact and protects the entire system.

Switches

RV accessories usually include switches, some of which should be replaced with heavier-duty models. Most switches are stamped 250VAC or 120VAC. They seldom bear DC ratings, but occasionally you will see a 24VDC designation. The 250VAC rating is the equivalent of a 24VDC rating.

Direct current produces an "arc" when a switch is turned on or off. This is especially true in motor-starting because of the large initial surge of current. Oversizing by using DC toggle switches (or

FIGURE 6.6: A combination AC/DC breaker/fuse panel with converter.

FIGURE 6.7: Bus conversions often have many more 12-volt circuits. This elaborate fuse/breaker center affords easy troubleshooting and protection. The more outlets, appliances, and equipment place a larger demand on the battery.

even regular or silent—but *not* mercury—household-type switches) works for the light-duty applications. This is a simple addition for lighting purposes. For heavy-duty loads, a "slave switch" can be installed. A light-duty wall switch activates a relay coil, and heavy relay contacts supply the DC load (Figure 6.8). Arcing at switches can be suppressed by installing capacitors and diodes.

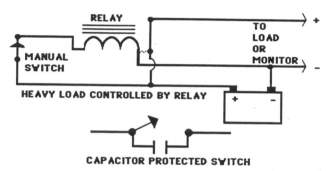

FIGURE 6.8: A heavy-duty relay between the battery and the load decreases the length of wire needed and thus increases efficiency.

Connectors and Terminals

Quality connections are important. A poor connection can lead to voltage drop and other problems. Connectors keep wires in contact with one another, under screw heads, and on terminal strips. They also help isolate positive and negative wires.

The two alternatives in making connections are soldering and crimp junctions. Crimp-on terminal connectors (Figure 6.9) are easy to use, the spade type being the handiest since it can be inserted under a screw head/washer without removing the screw

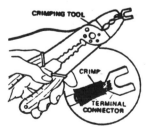

FIGURE 6.9: Attach terminal connectors with a crimping tool.

itself. Use a crimping tool and twist and pull the joint to make sure it is tight.

Protect your connections against corrosion. Battery acid can eat through a ring connector in a week or so. Salt water from road spray is also corrosive to copper joints. Use rubber or vinyl electrical tape to seal all joints. Silicone grease on battery terminals is an effective deterrent to corrosion.

Troubleshooting

Isolating the Open Circuit

If no voltage appears to be reaching an appliance, check the fuse panel first. Use your voltmeter. If you have labeled your fuse panel, it is easy to trace to where power originates. Otherwise, check power on the circuit side of the fuse panel for each fuse. Bad fuses may be identified by the appearance of burned fuse wires, but sometimes they melt at one end and still look perfectly good. Before replacing a fuse, know why it blew. A momentary short? An overload? Do not bypass fuses with foil or larger fuses. Correct the problem.

If the fuses check out okay, go to the appliance, outlet or light, and check again. Check for ground connection! Every "expert" has at one time disassembled a motor or an entire wiring system only to find that a simple ground wire, somewhere else, had been disconnected. Make sure that both positive and negative are actually available at the appliance.

Isolating a Short Circuit

In an electrical short circuit, positive will eventually connect in some way with negative. If a fuse continues to blow, you must locate where the two make contact because that is where the problem is.

When checking for shorts, first isolate the circuit, unplug all items, and remove covers at lamps and receptacles. Use a logical process of elimination to locate where continuity between (+) and (–) actually takes place. Sometimes a loose wire will have contacted ground at a socket where wires are very close together. The most difficult to find short I've encountered was caused by a screw in the outer skin of the RV which had penetrated a hidden positive wire. Finding it was just a matter of isolating one section at a time and checking each with an ohmmeter.

An ohmmeter will confirm a short. Disconnect your 12VDC, leaving ground alone (once you have determined that it is in fact grounded). Disconnect (+) at the main board and at the troublesome appliance. If you touch one test lead to ground and the other to the isolated wire, your meter should read infinite resistance. If your meter reads no resistance (or zero), you have a short. Examine the line one piece at a time, visually or in metered sections. Note particularly branches that "wander off" to other areas. Also note that some circuits actually make a loop of the RV and are connected to the 12 VDC supply in two places. Vibration in an RV may cause wire connections to work loose. Increased resistance due to a loose connection or corrosion may show voltage (continuity) on a meter without the ability to conduct amps. A 2-amp 12-volt test bulb (stop lamp with pigtails) will help detect this condition.

Inspect Wire Condition

Make sure that wiring is not frayed, twisted, or corroded. All positive wire connections must be insulated. Dogs and other animals have been known to strip the insulation from exposed wiring circuits—tail light, brake, and battery wires. Inspect these areas before a trip and during stays in remote areas.

While our RV was idle, pack rats entered service compartments through the wheel wells. They filled the converter compartment with cactus berries and chewed all the insulation from the copper wires. Had this happened while the wires were energized (or had we used the RV without checking it out), a fire could have occurred. Take precautions.

SOLAR SYSTEM INSTALLATION

Now that you are familiar with RV wiring and the operation of a solar system, it is time to determine the placement of your solar components within the RV. Installation involves the following basic steps:

1. arranging the solar panels and attaching them to the roof,
2. running the wire,
3. hooking up the control system (regulator/meters), and
4. attaching the charge wires to the battery.

It is a good idea to draw a layout diagram of your RV, as shown in Figure 6.10, and to "dry run" all steps before the actual installation. Make a careful plan whether you install the system or have it installed at a local solar or RV service center. Your system should be accompanied by a complete step-by-step instruction manual.

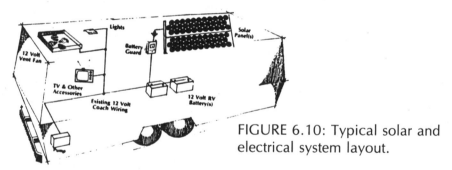

FIGURE 6.10: Typical solar and electrical system layout.

Solar Panel Placement

Proper placement of your solar panels on the RV roof is of critical importance to the functioning of your system. Although several steps precede the actual securing of solar panels to the roof, the bolting positions must be determined in advance. The panel mounting structure must be secured to the roof with screws long enough to attach to the wooden or metal framework, rafter, or other solid backing. On fiberglass-roofed RVs, plywood usually underlies the entire roof surface. In this case, you are free to secure

FIGURE 6.11: Four solar panel installation. Placing panels to avoid shadows from each other and roof-mounted structures (pod, air conditioner, antenna, vents) is important.

the panels in almost any location. Otherwise, locate and mark rafters for secure bolting sites. Be sure to check your layout diagram for potential internal wiring interference.

Possible mounting locations are illustrated in Figure 6.12. A single-panel mounting structure is narrow enough to fit alongside a vent or air conditioner. Dual-panel mounting can be accomplished by a side-by-side arrangement or end-to-end in a long narrow space.

Review the discussion on mounting and tilting considerations in chapter 5. A shadow on one solar cell will reduce the output of the entire panel. Locate panels to avoid shadows from the pod, roof vents, roof air conditioner, and TV antenna. Also, consider your parking preferences, especially for wintertime use. Will you need

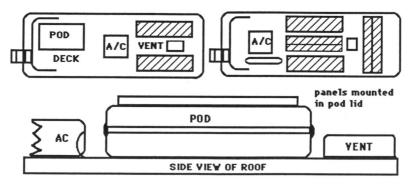

FIGURE 6.12: Possible mounting locations for solar panels on the RV roof.

to tilt your panels? Will there be any interference? Side-by-side mounting requires at least three feet between units to prevent winter shading from adjacent tilted panels.

A Typical System

Systems designed especially for RV applications are the easiest to install. For instruction purposes, we will illustrate the installation of our own prepackaged system, the RV POWERPAC. The general information, and most particulars, are applicable to all solar systems, but some details may vary. When installing, refer to your system's installation manual.

The RV POWERPAC ranges in size from one to four solar panels. The basic starter system (one-panel set-up), once installed, can be expanded up to four panels at any time, with no additional wiring. In addition to the solar panel and control system described in chapter 5, the system includes the following installation hardware:

- Dual-panel mounting frame, with end rails and mounting feet
- 30-foot wiring harness with UV-resistant cable cover
- Cable clamps and clips for strain relief
- Grommets and insulators with interconnecting wires
- Crimp terminal ends, screws and bolts
- Mastic sealer for mounting holes
- 25-amp fuse and holder to protect the charging circuit

The 30-foot length of wiring included with the system will be sufficient for most installations, but measure ahead of time to make sure your proposed wiring route will be accommodated. If it is longer, you will need to buy heavier wire for the entire system. Usually it is more practical to rearrange the location of the components. Instead of positioning the control system and the panels and batteries at opposite ends of the RV, plan for them to be closer. This increases efficiency and saves excess wire length.

The Necessary Tools

To install your system, you will need just a basic toolbox—pliers, Phillips screwdriver, wire cutter/stripper, pocket knife, pencil, and ladder. For fiberglass roofs, use a power drill for the mounting screw holes. For sheet metal roofs, an ice pick is the tool of choice.

Attach the Mounting Frames to the Solar Panels

First prepare a flat, cushioned surface upon which to safely lay the panels face down. Two mounting feet, or pads, are incorporated into each end of the mounting frame and are the avenues through which the screws attach the panel to the roof. The pads also provide space for air circulation which offsets decreased solar panel efficiency due to hot temperatures. To attach the mounting frames to the solar panels, see Figure 6.13 and follow these steps.

1. Attach the end rails on each end of the panels with 1/4-inch bolts and nuts so that the junction boxes on the panels match at each end (+ and +). The "L" flange of the rail must be mounted toward the end.
2. The previously determined location of the solar panels, according to rafters or other options, dictates the position of the mounting pads. Measure the area for accurate fit, and mark the area of the RV roof for mounting pad position.
3. The mounting pads can be positioned to mount 46- to 50-inch centers. Face the pads inward to shorten the distance, outward to lengthen the distance. A 48-inch center requires that one pad be turned inward, the other outward. (See Figure 6.14.)

FIGURE 6.13: Use nut, bolt, and lock washer to attach panels to the mounting frames.

FIGURE 6.14: Mounting pad position can lengthen or shorten the space between attachment holes, fit to the rafters.

Attach Wires to the Panel

This is easy. Just attach the wires inside the junction boxes on each end of the panel as shown in Figure 6.15: red wires to positive terminals, black wires to negative terminals.

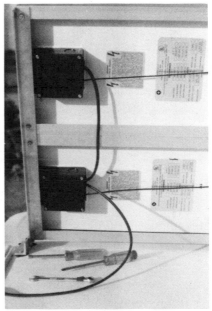

FIGURE 6.15: Wiring connections at the junction boxes make easy hook-up.

FIGURE 6.16: Panel mounting wires lead down the corner of the RV to the battery compartment. There is easy access for tilting when necessary.

FIGURE 6.17: Solar panels tilted for winter use. The shadow from the air conditioner will reduce the output of the shaded panel.

Secure the wire cable to the strain relief clamp on the panel frame. Where double panel arrangements are spaced on the roof, an interconnecting cable is run between the panel set-ups. In this way, additional panels can be added later just by attaching to the roof wiring. Don't cut interconnecting cables too short. Allow sufficient slack for tilting in either direction should the need arise.

Secure the Frame to the Roof

Position your panel in its preselected location. For a fiberglass roof, drill through the mounting pad holes with a 3/32-inch drill (Figure

6.18). For a metal roof, pierce with an ice pick into the support (Figure 6.19). Do not let the panel move as you drill or pierce the first hole. Start the screw to stabilize and then drill or pierce the second hole, and so on.

Pencil the outline of the mounting pads onto the roof so that the panels can be repositioned exactly after removing drill chips. Put a small piece of mastic sealer over each hole to act as a weatherproof seal and gasket. Place the panel over the prealigned pencil marks, insert screws, and tighten. For tilting, simply remove two bolts and insert a leg.

In situations where the roof is too weak, or drilling holes may void the manufacturer's warranty, it is possible to mount panels without even touching the roof's surface. Place two 8-foot lengths of 2-inch channel tubing across the roof, spaced about 4 feet apart. Attach tubing to the side of the RV with angle stock. The panels can then be mounted onto the channel tubing as you would to the roof.

FIGURE 6.18: Drill all holes with caution.

FIGURE 6.19: A pierced hole leaves better screw threading material in a metal roof.

Route Wires from the Panel to the Control Center

Routing wires from the solar panel to the regulator/meter center should also be planned. Figuring out how to route the cable from the outside to the inside of the RV requires a bit of ingenuity. Your diagram with dimensions will help you determine the most direct route.

A no-drill entry is preferable to punching holes in the RV roof. Ideally the cable should enter behind a cabinet within the RV. Our recommendation is to route the cable through the roof refrigerator vent, as shown in Figure 6.20. There is plenty of space behind the refrigerator to conceal the wiring and to avoid contact with heating elements. Many RVs have vinyl trim strips that can be removed and replaced. Another no-drill option is to enter through a rooftop sewer vent cap, which in most cases opens into an enclosed cabinet space.

FIGURE 6.20: Having the cable enter the RV through the refrigerator vent is a "no drill" entry.

Don't be tempted to wire-in at the converter. Because this center has its own function, it is best to go "direct" to the battery. If the no-drill alternatives above won't work in your situation, another simple solution is available. As shown in Figure 6.21 you can run the wire over the edge of the RV and through the side wall to allow entry into a cabinet.

FIGURE 6.21: Running the wire over the edge and then through the side wall will allow entry into a cabinet.

Be careful when drilling through walls and ceilings inside the RV (Figure 6.22). Turn the power off, drill a small hole first, and then enlarge after checking with a probe. Drilling into existing wiring or the water tank is no fun.

FIGURE 6.22: Routing wires through cabinets and behind furniture to conceal cable.

Install the Control Center and Make Battery Connections

Accessibility to your control center is important. A vertical surface at eye level is recommended for ease in meter reading. If you use the refrigerator vent for cable entry, the refrigerator wall is a logical

FIGURE 6.23: Compare the unsightly exposed wires on the left to the neatly concealed installation on the right.

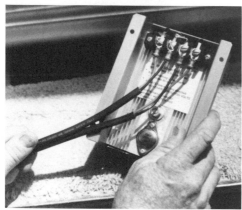

FIGURE 6.24: Making the connection to the control/regulator.

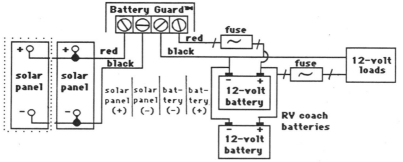

FIGURE 6.25: Typical solar system diagram. The control/meter center is located between the solar panels and the battery.

site for the regulator set-up. Cabinet mounting is ideal for conceal-ing wires (Figure 6.23).

As with any electrical equipment, some heat is generated by the regulator. Mount it on a wall or cabinet free of obstructions. Allow at least three inches of clearance top and bottom for air flow.

When the wiring harness and other components are color-coded, as in this system, connections are easy: red wire to positive, black to negative. Attach the spade terminals with crimping pliers. Figure 6.24 shows the connections on the back of the control center.

The parallel relationship of the control system, the solar panels, and the battery is illustrated in the schematic Figure 6.25. Run the wires to the battery compartment, and make all connec-tions in parallel: positive poles to positive, and negative poles to negative.

Installing a 25-amp fuse and fuse holder in the solar circuit near the battery will protect this circuit in the event of a short. Don't install "extras" in the charge line unless there is a specific reason. There is no point in running heavy cable and then interrupting it with #16 wire or flimsy contacts. The same applies to hooking up an ammeter. Make sure it is a good one and don't use teeny little slip-on connectors.

FIGURE 6.26: A wall-mounted BATTERY GUARD. A convenient location is important for ease in observation.

FIGURE 6.27: A BATTERY GUARD and TEST MODULE integrated with other wall-mounted components and gauges.

After installing your solar system, you will want to know that it is operating satisfactorily. Double-check the anchor bolts for tightness and see that all wires are secure. Seal well where wires enter the RV. Reread the operation manual to see that you understand how the equipment works, and make sure that everyone who operates the control reads it, too. Then sit back and relax as your RV battery gets its charge from sunlight.

7
DC–AC POWER INVERTERS

INTRODUCTION

At one time, we were trying to convert our blender, mixer, and an electric drill to run off 12 volts. What a job these conversions turned out to be! That was before we learned about 120-volt inverters. Since that discovery, we have tested and used many types of inverters in our RV: some with good results, others we wouldn't recommend under any circumstances.

Inverters have been used since World War II when Navy ships ran on DC power only. Any AC power that was needed was supplied by a rotary inverter (also called a motor/generator) located at the point of use. These rugged units were only about 50% efficient, but they did produce AC power. Our first inverter was the rotary type, durable, almost indestructible. It allowed us to use most of our AC appliances, but it did have a few drawbacks. It had poor efficiency and used extra energy to run its mechanical motor—over and above whatever the AC appliances required. The noise it made was similar to an electric motor, slightly irritating.

There was also a wide variation in the voltage and frequency range depending on the size of the load. We found some small loads ran faster than usual and some high-energy loads ran at a pace slower than normal.

For the past few years we have been using a solid-state TRACE Engineering inverter. All the disadvantages that we found in the rotary inverter have been eliminated in this new quiet model. In fact, we are so pleased with the ultra-high efficiency and reliable performance of the unit in our own RV that we consider it the ideal companion for other typical RV users.

You can now enjoy the convenience of 120-volt AC at a reasonable cost—whenever and wherever you want—without converting your appliances to 12 volt, running a gasoline generator, or having to seek park hook-ups.

Inverters depend on the battery for a reserve of energy. When the RV's service cord is plugged into the inverter, your RV's entire electric system is energized—driving down the road or parked in a remote spot.

In this section we will introduce you to the different types of inverters, and help you determine which type best suits your needs.

DO YOU NEED AN INVERTER?

If you run convenience appliances for less than 15 minutes at a time, an inverter can make your life easier. Loads run for 15 minutes or less are **short run loads**. Gasoline generators are best suited for **heavy loads**, especially ones run for long periods of time (hours). Now with high-efficiency equipment, you can run even long-running heavy loads effectively: a load of 250 watts for four or five hours can use one battery-full of power (250 watts × 4 hr = 1000 watt hours or 1 full battery).

Most motorhomes come equipped with a large engine generator for running the roof air conditioner, icemaker, and other heavy loads. The generator will last longer if you save it for these loads and use a 1200-watt inverter to provide the quiet AC power for all the small load, instant-use items. It is especially ideal during "quiet hour" when no one wants a generator running. For trailer owners, it certainly isn't convenient to get the portable generator out and fire it up just to make a couple slices of toast or to drill a few holes. The inverter offers instant power—when you want it, ever so quietly. That's the real convenience, 24 hours a day.

You must ask yourself if the convenience the AC equipment offers justifies inclusion in your RV system and your lifestyle. We personally enjoy the microwave oven and VCR late at night, a time when running the generator would be offensive to our neighbors.

To determine whether an inverter will work for you, you need to calculate the watt ratings of the loads you plan to use. You need to determine how you will recharge the batteries. Do you presently have a generator that can power these loads? We will address these matters in later sections.

What Can You Operate With your High-Efficiency Inverter?

Any AC appliance or tool can be operated with a high-efficiency inverter with modified sine wave output: microwave ovens, blenders, refrigerators, skill saws, vacuum cleaners, TVs, VCRs.

You must size the inverter to the surge requirements of starting induction-type motors, like those found in refrigerators or pumps. These unusual loads require up to seven times the rating of the running amps. That's why the inverter you select must have good surge capability.

For example, say you want to operate a 400-watt freezer that needs a six times surge to start. It would require a 2400-watt *surge* (400 × 6 = 2400 watts). Compare this to the rating on the inverter.

INVERTER BENEFITS

The primary benefit of an inverter-powered AC system is the convenience of instant reliable power, without the noise, fumes, and vibration of the gasoline or diesel generator. Because RVs (motorhomes and tow rigs) are already equipped with a 100+ horsepower power plant (the vehicle's engine) and battery charging capability via the alternator, an inverter eliminates the need to run the generator most of the time. With a properly sized battery bank and high-output alternator or solar panels, small RVs can eliminate the generator entirely.

For motorhomes already equipped with a generator for running roof air conditioners, the inverter will serve several purposes:

1. Reduce generator running time to an absolute minimum, thereby increasing the life of the generator.
2. Reduce the low power use of the generator which, manufacturers are quick to warn, will cause excess carbon build-up on valves and other problems from its running at a fraction of its rated output.
3. Allow 120-volt AC appliances to be run after "quiet hour."
4. Increase the overall self-sufficiency of the RV's power usage since the inverter only draws the power needed by the appliance. Generators, of course, operate at a certain rpm and consume a certain amount of fuel (while using up its life hours) regardless of the load.

Most RVs already have a good battery system with deep-cycle batteries that should be able to handle light to medium AC loads for "on board" convenience. However, your battery/inverter system should *not* be expected to run the extremely high energy demand that refrigerators, roof air conditioners, or even icemakers require. These loads are best left to electrical hook-ups or big generators. This is not to say that an inverter cannot run these loads, but the many extra batteries required to store the vast amount of power necessary would not be practical or cost-effective.

HOW AN INVERTER WORKS

A solid-state inverter uses pairs of switching transistors or SCRs to shift the DC current through a large transformer (see Figure 7.1). The control circuits are very sensitive and determine the precise

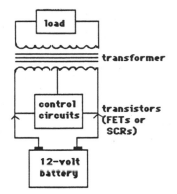

FIGURE 7.1: The transformer in the inverter works much like the gears in a car. It changes 12 volt to 120 volt, comparing high rpm/low torque to low rpm/higher torque—a ratio of 1:10.

time to switch, adjusting the quality of power desired by the load. Some models use field effect transistors (FET) switching devices. They act more rapidly than SCRs and help maintain a very high degree of efficiency over the entire output range. That they have fewer major parts means that reliability may be higher: fewer things to go wrong. FETS are very fast operating devices, therefore the circuits that protect the inverter need to be faster still. Excellent engineering design is necessary for these units to be reliable and consistent. Control circuits are one area where high-tech electronics is making great strides by developing high efficiency and better wave form for operating all varieties of appliances.

Operation

When the inverter is first hooked up the power switch should be "off." The inverter will automatically shut down if an overload situation is created by over-current, high or low battery voltage, or excess heat build-up in the transformer or heat sink.

Indicator Lights

ON/OFF: Lights when you first turn the unit on to indicate operation.

OVERLOAD: Indicates when the situation arises that the inverter must protect itself from any of the conditions mentioned above.

This protection is controlled by sensors that compensate for heat build-up as well as unusual over-current situations.

CHARGING LAMP: Indicates that the battery is being charged due to the presence of 120VAC from an outside source (park power or generator).

TYPES OF INVERTER LOADS

Resistive Loads are loads that produce heat—light bulbs and heating elements. Since voltage and current are in phase, inverters drive these loads easily and efficiently.

Inductive Loads include induction motors (those without brushes) and transformers (found in most electronic devices: TVs, stereos, microwave ovens, etc.). Current is out of phase with voltage and continues to enter the inverter after the voltage has stopped; the way the inverter handles this delayed voltages affects its efficiency. These loads prefer the purest form of sine wave: short of this, reducing distortion is paramount. A high-quality inverter uses a fast switching device to charge a capacitor and to feed back out-of-phase power as a boost. SCR-type inverters act too slowly. The lowest percent of distortion (10% down to 1% desired) is best.

Induction motors require up to six times their running current to start. Testing will determine which loads can be started and for how long they can be run. If a motor does not start within a few seconds, or if it begins to lose power after running a while, turn it off to avoid overheating.

Considerations

Reactive Loads: When operating motors, an electrical condition occurs that causes power to be fed back into the inverter. Through this effect, some inverters lose the ability to start large motors. High-quality inverters have special circuitry that assists in motor starting.

Power Factor: Distortion results when reactive loads are observed on the wave form. The windings in the motor cause interference in the current as the voltage rises and falls. While voltage is unaffected by the inductance, current has to work harder to keep in phase and so lags behind, needlessly wasting power. The difference between the amount of power available to the amount actually working is the loss. Some induction motors have power factors of 0.7, meaning that they only consume 70% of the power available. Select a motor with a high power factor, like 0.9.

A sophisticated inverter will handle this reflected power feedback by having an electrical storage capacitor across the inductive load. The capacitor has an opposite effect and helps maintain the load at high output.

Problem Loads

Very Small Loads: If an appliance consumes less power than the "turn on point" of the inverter, then you may momentarily turn on another load to help start the inverter.

Fluorescent Lights & Power Supplies: Some equipment cannot be detected by the inverter's load sensor. (Though with fluorescents, altering plug polarity, i.e., turning the plug over, could help.) Some computers and electronics do not present a load until the line voltage is available. In these situations, the device is waiting for the inverter to begin while the inverter is waiting for the device. Add a small companion load (a light or appliance) momentarily to initiate inverter start-up.

Microwave Ovens: These devices are sensitive to peak output voltage: the higher the voltage, the faster they cook. Grid power has higher peak voltage than inverter power whose voltage depends on battery voltage and load. If battery voltage is low, cooking time will be increased.

Clocks: Though clocks usually do not draw sufficient power to activate the inverter, it is preferable to use battery-operated clocks. Inverter-operated clocks do not keep proper time. Use them only if they are included in your appliances, but compensate for the fast or slow difference.

Electronics: AM radios are likely to pick up inverter-induced noise. A filter capacitor may help in some instances. Computers should not be run while large loads are being started to avoid head crash problems or noise.

Low Battery: If your batteries can't deliver the amperage necessary to drive a load without dropping below 10 volts, the inverter will turn off to protect the batteries. Table 7.1 can be used to help estimate battery requirements.

Table 7.1: Watts Out vs Time vs Battery Drain

Load (watts)	Load (amps)	Typical Device	Time (min)				
			5	15	30	60	120
			amp hours used				
30	0.3	stereo	0.2	0.6	1.4	2.7	5.4
60	0.5	TV (B&W)	0.5	1.4	2.7	5.4	10.9
100	0.9	computer	0.8	2.3	4.5	9.1	18.1
200	1.7	TV (color)	1.5	4.5	9.0	18.1	36.3
400	3.4	blender	3.0	9.1	18.1	36.3	72.5
800	6.8	skill saw	6.0	18.1	36.3	72.5	145.0
1000	8.5	toaster	7.6	22.7	45.3	90.6	181.3
1200	10.3	microwave	9.3	27.8	55.6	111.1	222.2
1800	15.4	hot plate	14.5	43.5	87.1	174.2	348.4

*Courtesy Trace Engineering

INVERTER POWER RATINGS

There are three power ratings for inverters (engine-type generators use the same ratings).

Continuous Watt rating refers to the ability to supply power hour after hour without going into overload. For 12-volt inverters, the maximum output per inverter is limited to 2000 watts. The higher rating requires plenty of battery power to supply the inverter so to maintain maximum output without the battery falling below the cut-off level.

Intermittent Overload rating is usually limited to just a few minutes before the transformer and components become warm enough to kick on the overload protection. Some inverters can operate for 10 to 15 minutes in this overloaded stage, with loads twice the continuous rating. A quality inverter is protected from harm by protective, automatic turn-off features.

Surge Load is one of the most critical ratings. A surge load occurs when the load (motor) is turned "on" and a rush of current is required to get things going. AC motors are notoriously inefficient and this momentary surge of power can last up to a second, until the motor achieves running speed. The inverter must be sized to match anticipated surge loads. Compressors, pumps, and blowers are hard to start and may require up to seven times their running ratings. Ultra-high efficiency inverters are expensive, but they do allow good surge. Heart and Trace inverters, for example, provide short, strong pulses which lengthen as the load comes up to speed. If the load is so large the inverter can't come up to speed, it turns itself off in 15 seconds. This action allows the inverter to start loads many times larger than previously possible, while still giving short-circuit protection.

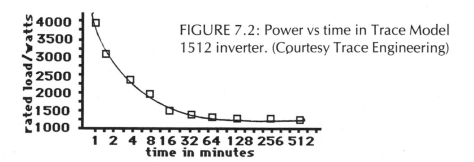

FIGURE 7.2: Power vs time in Trace Model 1512 inverter. (Courtesy Trace Engineering)

Table 7.2: Power Needed to Start Electric Motor (watts)

Motor Rating (hp)	Running Watts (approx)	Universal Motor	Induction Motor	Capacitor Motor
1/8	275	400	600	850
1/8	415	625	1037	1660
1/4	400	500	850	1050
1/4	600	900	1500	2400
1/3	450	600	975	1350
1/3	675	1015	1690	2700
1/2	600	750	1300	1800
1/2	900	1350	2250	3600
3/4	850	1000	1900	2600
3/4	1275	1915	3185	5100
1	1000	1250	2300	3000
1	1500	2250	3750	6000

TYPES OF INVERTERS

Square Wave inverters are only useful for certain types of loads, such as tape recorders and sewing machines—loads with small brush-type motors. Square wave inverters are not recommended for use with color TVs, induction motors, and similar loads since the wave form is distorted and causes overheating. These inverters are available in sizes ranging from 50 to 1000 watts. Unfortunately, they have a tendency to self-destruct, and they also draw three to four amps at no-load.

Sine Wave power is produced by a rotating armature, like the power produced by the utilities or a generator. Rotary inverters have a powerful DC motor to turn a generator. They are very effective in running motors and transformers. Frequency and voltage vary with the battery voltage, depending on the load applied. There is a loss of efficiency due to mechanical conversion. Surgeability is no better than that of fuel-powered generators.

Modified Sine Waves are produced electronically. The pulse width is varied to suit the load. Frequency and voltage are precisely maintained by control circuits. There are no limitations on the type of load. High efficiency models are available that convert up to 93% of the energy supplied to working energy. Higher efficiency means less heat is generated. Surgeability reaches to 300% of continuous rating.

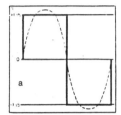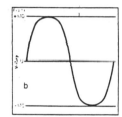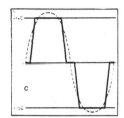

FIGURE 7.3: a. Square Wave. b. Sine Wave. c. Modified Sine Wave.

INVERTER EFFICIENCY

Inverter efficiency is very important to the RVer. Since the inverter depends on battery power, it is critical that you not waste energy. Efficiency is the ratio of power *in* to power *out*. If you put in 100 watts of power and receive only 50 watts out, you are working at 50% efficiency. The other 50%, in inverter use, is wasted as heat. Most inverters have a peak efficiency of about 80% of capacity. When using a large inverter for small loads, the efficiency is usually poor (40% or less). An ultra-high efficiency inverter can have good effective power over the entire power range. This high efficiency pays off by having the ability to change the energy from your battery and convert it to usable AC power without heat (loss) being generated.

An example of power conversion: At 100% efficiency, an inverter would yield 1 amp of AC power if 10 amps of DC current were taken from the battery—a ratio of 1:10. At 75% efficiency, the 10-amp draw gives 0.75 amp AC power.

Battery power must be used as efficiently by the appliance as well. Let's assume we have 400 ampere hours of battery power. If the inverter is only 50% efficient (like a rotary inverter), there would only be 200 ampere hours of effective battery storage, the rest

Table 7.3: Inverter Comparison Chart

Selected Model Specifications	Mechanical	Electronic/Transformer		
		FET Hi-Efficiency	SCR Technology	Silicon Transistor
Technology Feature of Operation	Motor/Generator Mechanical DC motor/ AC generator	Low power required to operate special transistors.	Requires extra energy to produce AC output.	Frequency controlled mode requires extra energy to produce AC output.
Rated Watts Output				
Continuous	1600 watts	2000 watts	1800 watts	1000 watts
10-min. overload	1700 watts	2500 watts	2000 watts	Not recommended
Surge above cont. output	28%	300% (4000 watts)	85%	10%
Range of Operation (min. to max. amps AC)	9–15	0–16	0–15	0–8.5
Output Voltage	104–127 V unregulated	120 V regulated 2%	120 V regulated 2%	Voltage varies direct to battery voltage
Frequency at 60 HZ	60–70 Hz depending on load	0.1% at 60 Hz	0.1% at 60Hz	2% at 60 Hz
Electronic Overload Protection	Circuit breaker only	Full protection	Full protection	Circuit breaker only
Power Factor	Good	Excellent 1 to 0.1 lag	Fair to 0.7 lag	Med/low to 0.8 lag
Overall Efficiency	Low	Excellent	Moderate	Fair
Highest Efficiency	64% at 80% load	94% at only 10% load	82% at 85% load	56% at 75% load
No-Load Idle Current	4 amps DC	0.07 amps DC	2 amps DC	3.5 amps DC
Wave Form Output	sine wave (pure)	modified sine wave	modified square wave	square wave
Approx. Cost	$900	$1200	$1100	$600
Recommended Usage	When abundant DC supply (while charging). Use with 9 to 15 amp load. Not electronics or sensitive appliances.	With any load from computers & VCRs to difficult to start induction motors. Operates wide range of small appliances to large motors with effectiveness.	Best with loads of 800 to 1400 watts. Transformers or induction motors may overheat or lose strength. Microwaves require longer cooking time.	Not recommended for induction/capacitor motors or sensitive loads. Induction motors and transformers overheat. AC voltage output depends on battery voltage.

would be lost as heat. If I use this power for 15 minutes of cooking in the microwave and 10 minutes with the curling iron or 1 hour of TV, I could extend these times to nearly twice as long *on the same power* if I use an inverter that is 95% efficient. You need less recharging equipment and batteries when the inverter and the appliances are of the highest efficiency.

CRITERIA FOR HIGH-EFFICIENCY INVERTER DESIGN

A reliable inverter depends on careful design of circuits, rapid protection circuitry, and sound construction. The protective circuitry monitors battery voltage (high or low), AC circuit overload, temperature rise and other technical surges that the components are subject to. Low voltage doesn't harm the inverter but could deplete the battery if there is a continued down draw. High battery voltages can cause high voltage spikes that may affect sensitive electronic equipment, therefore the inverter shuts down to prevent damage. Overcurrent protection is triggered when the demands exceed the safe operation of the transistors. Thermal protection is observed constantly in the transistor's heat sink and the transformer

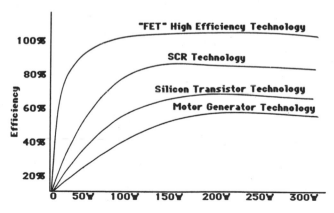

FIGURE 7.4: Comparisons of efficiency vs output for various types of inverter technology. Operating efficiency below 50% is unacceptable for any length of time. You will run out of battery power.

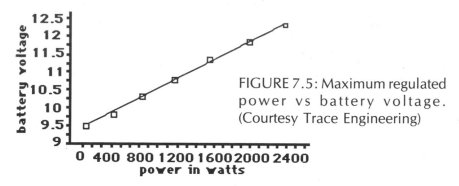

FIGURE 7.5: Maximum regulated power vs battery voltage. (Courtesy Trace Engineering)

windings. The temperature sensors also compensated for output and wave form changes as the transistors warm up. The power a semiconductor can handle is dependent upon the rise of temperature so the protection plan adjusts the output threshold according to what power will be safe to deliver.

QUALITY AND CONTROL OF OUTPUT POWER

The quality of power produced by the inverter is one factor that can mean the difference between satisfaction and dissatisfaction. Clean usable power is what you want. The wave form closest to sine wave is most desirable. Modified sine waves produced by a quality inverter can be used by all types of equipment even if used with sensitive electronic equipment. More on wave form later.

Voltage Regulation

Precise voltage regulation ensures that the power to the load remains consistent regardless of fluctuations in battery voltage. This is absolutely necessary for electronic equipment, like computers. Rotary-type inverters do not have voltage regulation.

Frequency Regulation

Frequency-sensitive electronic equipment like VCRs, computers, and color TVs require 60 Hz. Frequency regulation is only avail-

able on solid-state inverters. They use a crystal control with toler-
ance of ± 1% at 60 Hz.

*   *   *

The closer the quality of your power is to that of utility power, the
better. If you only want to use a blender, vacuum cleaner or hair
dryer, then you can use just about any type of inverter. In fact, since
those appliances do not require pure quality power, you should
buy the cheapest inverter you can find. Induction motors require
good quality power. Efficiency with various types of loads requires
a good power match. If you plan to use a microwave oven, electric
typewriter, VCR, color TV or any electronic equipment, then you
need a regulated source that will work efficiently. When your
computer is run from an inverter, it becomes an uninterruptible
power supply. It cannot be affected by brown outs, surges, spikes
or any of the other disturbances utility power would experience.

AC LOAD PLANNING AND SWITCHING

AC hook-up can be arranged through automatic switch relays,
manual transfer switches, or simply by using a line cord and
receptacle. These methods allow loads to be run from generator,
utility/shore power or from an inverter.

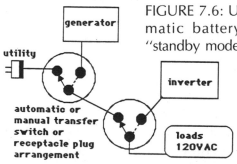

FIGURE 7.6: Use of a transfer switch. An automatic battery charger is wired into the
"standby model" inverter with a built-in transfer switch. The output from
the generator and inverter
should *never* be hooked
together. Wiring in special
circuits for a split system may
require the services of an
electrician.

INVERTER SIZING AND SELECTION

The size of your inverter will be determined by:

1. Continuous running watts of the loads
2. Surge power required
3. Quality of power (wave form and regulation) required
4. Efficiency of operation
5. Options and safety features

Selecting an inverter is simple if you follow these basic rules.

How to Size an Inverter

Make a list of all the equipment you are likely to run at one time and add up the wattages. Wattage information should appear on a label on the equipment. If it doesn't, consult the "AC Appliance Load Guide" below for approximate figures. Be sure to consider all possible combinations.

Match your maximum figure to the inverter manufacturer's ratings. For example, if the computer takes 100 watts, the monitor 40 watts, and the printer 110 watts, that's a total of 250 watts. This combination could be operated from a 300-watt or larger inverter.

Next determine surge requirements for the AC motors. Some motors require up to seven times the running wattage. Talk to the technical department of the inverter manufacturer if a critical item, like a deep-freeze or a compressor motor, comes close to the upper limit.

Select an inverter with a wattage rating greater than the wattage you need to power your largest load.

Power Quality Considerations

The quality of power produced by the inverter is a major consideration. Simple brush-type motors can be operated on an inexpensive square wave inverter, but induction motors and transformers or color TVs require less distortion, and the voltage/frequency control that comes from a more refined inverter—modified sine wave.

Efficiency

Efficiency is tied to how much battery storage you can carry in the RV. If you have lots of extra batteries (which I doubt you do), efficiency is no problem. However, the typical RVer should select the inverter with the highest efficiency available—over the entire power range—making it ideal for all sized items.

AC Appliance Load Guide
(see page 142)

You may use any combination of appliances at one time as long as the total load does not exceed the maximum rated output of the inverter. Lighter loads may be run from a larger inverter. An overload of 10 to 15% can usually be tolerated for 5 to 15 minutes before shutdown. Long-running equipment (*) benefits from an inverter with a wide high-efficiency range to gain maximum running time from the same battery power.

Inverter Options

Inverter options include built-in chargers, remote power centers, stacking or synchronizing capability, special indicator lights, and external cooling fans. Each option increases the price slightly. Safety protection features include low battery cut-off, high battery cut-off, circuit breaker protection, thermal cut-out, and time delay shut-off from over-surge motor starting. These standard features add to the cost, but protect the expensive inverter and other equipment from harm.

AC Appliance Load Guide

AC Appliance	Label Watts	12VDC Amps from Battery
Light Loads—Use 300-watt or larger inverter		
1.4-in. electric drill	300	30
Electric razor	30	3
*Stereo turntable	100	10
*Satellite TV system	250	25
*Stereo	15	1.5
Large light bulb	100	10
Kitchen blender	300	30
*Computer	100	10
*Printer	110	11
12-in. TV (B&W)	55	5.5
19-in. TV (color)	100	10
Electric broom (15 min)	350	35
*Electric typewriter	150	15
Sewing machine	150	15
Hair clippers	75	7.5
Fan (16-in.)	250	25
VCR	90	9
Medium to Heavy Loads—Use 1200- to 2000-watt inverter (Add 10% for internal inverter loss)		
10-in. rock cutting saw	600	60
*Coffee maker	700	70
Electric iron or toaster	900	90
1/2-in. electric drill	600	60
Slide projector	600	60
Microwave oven (600 w mag.)	1200	120
Full-size vacuum	1100	110
Electric chain saw	1200	120
Skill saw	1100	110
Hair dryer/blower	1200	120
Hair curlers	600	60
Waffle iron	900	90
*Refrigerator/ice maker	700+	70

*Long-running equipment benefits from an inverter with a wide range and high-efficiency to gain maximum running time from the same battery power.

Built-In Chargers (Stand-by Option)

This built-in feature is automatically activated by the internal transfer switch. When utility power or your generator AC power is available the unit operates as a highly effective battery charger while all loads are transferred to the incoming AC line. When the AC line is disconnected (the generator turned off), the unit returns to the inverter mode without interruption. Adjustable settings allow rapid recharging or low level "float" charging.

Built-In Meters

Observing the values of charging amps, battery voltage or AC input/output are important in understanding your electrical system, especially when troubleshooting a problem.

Remote Power Center

Use of this small attractive operating panel allows monitoring and control of the inverter from a convenient location up to 20 feet (or farther) away. The Trace inverter has a digital meter that is available at the panel that indicates conditions from inside the RV while the actual inverter is tucked away in an outside compartment.

Synchronous (Stacking or Cascading) Features

Modular inverters can be used as building blocks to create a larger output or when 220VAC is needed in a special application. Interfacing equipment and cables tie the inverters together so they synchronize cycles acting as one unit in unison. Batteries become very critical in these larger systems with high demand.

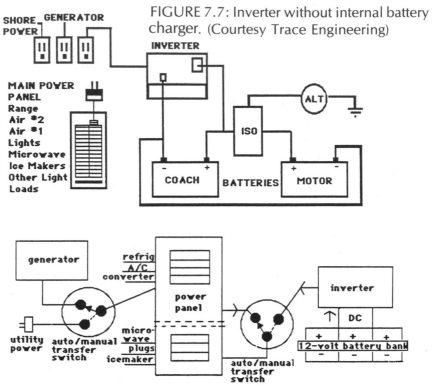

FIGURE 7.7: Inverter without internal battery charger. (Courtesy Trace Engineering)

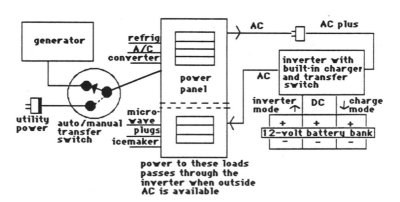

FIGURE 7.8: Automatic operation of an inverter without a built-in battery charger.

FIGURE 7.9: Automatic operation of an inverter with a built-in charger and transfer switch.

What Makes An Inverter Good

In order to get the most benefit from your inverter, it must meet several specific tests. Consider these when making your selection.

1. Must be *user friendly*. Some makes of equipment have hidden controls or settings, inside fuses, or awkward design that makes the unit difficult to operate. Keep it simple.
2. Good *surgeability*. Needed for starting AC motors. Some motors require up to 700% of running load to get started. High-quality inverters surge to 300% of rated output.
3. *Reliability*. If it doesn't operate, you get no work done.
4. *Efficiency*. Energy is expensive—you need to maximize what you've got. If the inverter is efficient, you will get more range out of a measured amount of battery power, and the battery will last longer.
5. *Factory service*. A readily available phone number is a great help in obtaining answers to technical questions from the trained staff.

Serious thought given to which inverter and what size inverter best suits your needs will save you from problems later.

CONNECTING THE INVERTER TO YOUR SYSTEM

Install the inverter in a dry, protected, and ventilated area. Place it as close to the batteries as you can to keep the cable runs short. Batteries emit corrosive fumes that should be considered when locating the inverter.

It is simple to hook-up an inverter. The power supply comes from the coach battery. There are only two wires involved. The POS (+) and NEG (−) wires that fasten to the terminals on the back of the unit need to be quite large, like welding cable. The RV's "shore cable" can be plugged into the inverter outlets so that all the plugs in your RV are energized. That's it.

FIGURE 7.10: An inverter plugged into a system.

BATTERIES FOR THE INVERTER SYSTEM

Inverters use battery power to produce 120 volts AC. A rapid drain is placed on the battery when 100 to 150 amps are demanded for long periods of time. Deep-cycle batteries are designed to be discharged more slowly than automotive starting batteries that deliver 500 amps for 10 seconds. Deep-cycle batteries are designed to discharge at a rate of 10 to 20% of their ampere-hour rating. To achieve a 100-amp sustained discharge from deep-cycle batteries, it would be ideal to have 5 batteries hooked in parallel: 5 batteries × 20% = 100 amps. If the load is to be used for 15 minutes or less, we can get by with fewer batteries.

To estimate battery drain, use the formulas in chapter 3.

Battery Bank Sizing

Add the daily ampere hours listed for your 12-volt appliances to that used by the 120-volt AC equipment to calculate your daily consumption. Multiply the ampere hours by 6 to arrive at the suggested battery size in ampere hours. Example: 15 AH from DC + 18 AH through the inverter = 33 AH consumed, so you'll need

198 AH of battery or two RV/marine batteries, sized at 105 AH each.

AC inverters require sufficient amps for maximum load sizing. If you expect to use a heavy load for extended periods, expect to need more batteries. If the AC loads are light and infrequent, then undersizing will usually be ok, but not recommended.

Recall that if a battery is continually discharged at a high rate, only part of the battery is used before the effective voltage drops off, thus limiting the available power. The solution to this is to use multiple batteries.

Battery Sizing Information for Inverter Users

To use an inverter to full advantage requires having batteries with good amperage output and with plenty of reserve power. It is best to select RV, marine or golfcart batteries that are deep-cycle batteries. Deep-cycles are made to be discharged deeply and then recharged on a daily basis without internal damage, unlike what would happen to an automotive-type battery.

When operating your inverter in the lower power ranges of 200 to 300 watts, you can get by with having only one battery. But to use the inverter to full advantage more batteries are needed to meet the demand. A microwave oven requires drawing nearly 100 amps from the battery (watts ÷ volts = amps). With this heavy load you will do well to have 300 to 400 amp hours or more of battery storage (each battery has about 100 amp hours of capacity).

Even a good quality battery that is full can only sustain a heavy load for a short period of time, but using more than one battery offers extended use time and better surge power when it is necessary.

6-Volt Golfcart or 12-Volt RV/Marine Batteries

Both of these batteries offer the same energy per pound of battery weight. Two 12-volt batteries connected in parallel gives 210 ampere hours at 12 volts; two 6-volt golfcart batteries in series is the same as 210 ampere hours at 12 volts. The problem occurs when you have to replace a single 6-volt battery. The newer battery can only deliver as much power as will pass through the older battery. Therefore, 12-volt units are more easily obtained, cost less, have fewer connections and get new life when replacing a single unit in parallel. Replace 6-volt batteries in pairs only.

HELPFUL HINTS AND TROUBLESHOOTING

Most inverter problems stem from locating the inverter too far from the battery, undersizing the wires, and overloading the inverter. Keep the inverter within 10 feet of the battery, using large wire (1/0 ga. or larger for 1200-watt models). Then you can run the AC wire for longer distances, since it has a higher voltage and less amperage to allow voltage drop. (AC has only one-tenth the amperage of low-voltage DC.)

Interference is caused by stray magnetic fields from wires, brushes or generating equipment that usually become apparent on radio or video equipment. Filters at the source or at the appliance can help eliminate these elusive problems. Check at a radio shop as to where filters should be used. Also improper grounding of the system can cause interference. Battery ground (negative) should be connected to the RV chassis (if a negative ground system).

Check the specifications of AC equipment to determine the wattage and surge load. These must match within the capability of the inverter and the battery supply system to operate satisfactorily.

The performance of the inverter is dependent upon the condition and ability of the battery bank to supply sufficient amps at the correct voltage while equipment is being operated. Proper selection and plenty of reserve is extremely important to achieve satisfactory results for the various power system. Check batteries independently rather than as a group.

USING AN INVERTER DOES NOT REQUIRE
SOLAR PANELS

Solar panels are not the only way batteries can be charged. An RV equipped with an inverter may be able to operate just fine on the charge derived from the automotive alternator. Keep in mind that batteries sometimes take hours to recharge, so driving often and for some distance may be necessary. If you seek hook-ups daily, the converter can also contribute to the charge.

FIGURE 7.11: How the system works. Everything revolves around the battery. Many recharging methods are available to an RV. The inverter is just a link from the battery to the AC system.

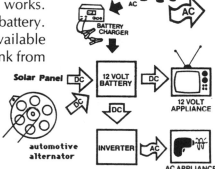

Appendix A
SOLAR CELL TECHNOLOGY

Photo is the Greek word for light, and *voltaic* refers to voltage or electricity. Photovoltaics is the process by which light is converted directly into electricity, a phenomenon achieved by the use of photovoltaic (or solar) cells.

Silicon dioxide (or quartz, SiO_2) is the second most abundant element on the earth's crust. As sunlight strikes an active silicon surface, billions of energy-carrying photons react each second. About 10 to 15% of the energy is converted to electricity, about 40% is absorbed as heat, and the other 50% is reflected. Different forms of silicon can be used to make solar cells. Because of its high efficiency and proven long life, single-crystal silicon remains the preferred material for solar cell production.

Research, improved production methods, and automation have reduced costs from $2000 per watt in 1958 to the relatively stable $9 per watt in 1993. It is hoped that this trend will continue.

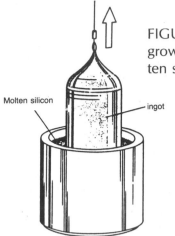

FIGURE A.1: The Czochralski method of growing an ingot from a crucible of molten silicon.

Molten silicon

ingot

FIGURE A.2:
A polycrystalline cell
in cross-section.

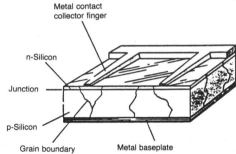

Metal contact
collector finger

n-Silicon

Junction

p-Silicon

Grain boundary

Metal baseplate

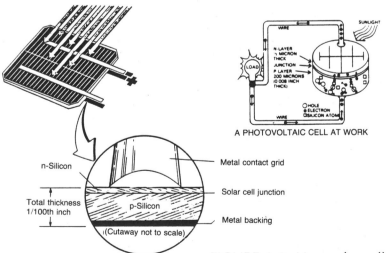

n-Silicon

Total thickness
1/100th inch

p-Silicon

(Cutaway not to scale)

Metal contact grid

Solar cell junction

Metal backing

A PHOTOVOLTAIC CELL AT WORK

FIGURE A.3: How solar cells work.

SINGLE-CRYSTAL SOLAR CELLS

To make single-crystal silicon cells, silicon dioxide is melted in a carbon arc furnace and transformed into semiconductor-grade silicon—the pure silicon used for making transistors and integrated circuits. Then a minute amount of boron is added to the hyper-pure molten silicon, and a single perfect tetrahedral crystal is "drawn" upward by freezing onto a slowly rotating seed crystal. It takes about 10 hours for this carefully controlled "Czochralski process" to produce an ingot 3 feet long by 2 to 5 inches in diameter, at a cost of about $100 to $200 per pound.

High-speed diamond saws slice the ingot into 0.015-inch wafers, or cells, cutting away about 40% of the precious silicon as dust in the process. Microscopic pyramids are etched onto the surface to increase (to about 85%) the cells' capabilities to absorb light energy. A second impurity, phosphorus, is added while the wafers are heated in a controlled furnace. Thus, two layers of silicon constitute a solar cell—one containing boron (the p-type layer), the other phosphorus (the sensitive, electron-rich n-type layer). The inequality of electrons in these two materials causes the movement of electrons from one layer to the other when exposed to light energy (photons). A grid of 44 electrical contacts is printed onto the phosphorus-treated surface to enable the free electrons in the silicon to "flow" into wires for transfer to a battery or load.

COMPETING TECHNOLOGIES

Polycrystalline silicon is less expensive to produce than single-crystal silicon, and because of the rectangular shape of the poly ingot, wafers can be packed more densely into a solar panel. Since a shorter time is devoted to cooling the molten silicon, the ingot is composed of microscopic crystals rather than the single large crystal that results from slow cooling. Free electrons moving within the silicon are detoured along grain boundaries while trying to reach the metal contact. This internal short circuiting reduces the efficiencies of polycrystalline silicon, especially when the sun is less than fully bright.

Much research is being conducted on **amorphous** (or thin-film) **silicon**. In this process, the cells are made by depositing an ultra-thin film of molten silicon onto a sheet of glass or stainless steel which is then cut to size. Amorphous cells are in great evidence powering small devices such as watches and calculators. Small panels are available for consumer use. The future of the technology is promising.

Solar cells are unique. They are hard-working devices that, when properly protected against moisture and impact, will last indefinitely. Environmentally sound, no materials are consumed, no emissions given off as solar cells silently and efficiently produce energy. *Practical Photovoltaics* by Richard Komp is highly recommended to anyone interested in a more in-depth examination of solar cell technology and its applications (see Appendix B).

Appendix B
RESOURCE LIST

MANUFACTURERS AND SUPPLIERS

This is a general listing of manufacturers to help get you started. It is not meant to be all-inclusive. Many brands--Koolatron, Sanyo, TMK, Honda, and Kawasaki, for example--are available just about everywhere.

Alternators

Central Hi-Power
910 East Willow
Long Beach CA 90706
213/427 6813

Delco Productions
Division of GM
Dayton OH 45401
513/455 5000

Lestek Manufacturing Inc.
6452 Baker Boulevard
Ft. Worth TX 76118
1/800 433 7628

TNT Electric
611 East Wayne Street
Fort Wayne IN 46802

Wrangler Power Products
PO Box 10005
Scottsdale AZ 85271
1/800 962 2616

Battery Chargers

Marquette Lincoln Automotive
St. Louis MO 63120
1/800 245 3862

Shauer Manufacturing
4500 Alpine Avenue
Cincinnati OH 45242
513/791 3030

Todd Engineering
28706 Holiday
Elkhart IN 46517
219/293 8633

Catalogs
Camping World
PO Box 90017
Bowling Green KY 42102
1/800 626 5944

J. C. Whitney & Co.
1917-19 Archer Avenue
PO Box 8410
Chicago IL 60680

RV Wholesalers
8978 West 7 Mile
Northville MI 48167

Converters
B-W Manufacturers
PO Box 739
Kokomo IN 46901

Newmark Products
10648 South Painter Avenue
Santa Fe Springs CA 90670

Todd Engineering
28706 Holiday
Elkhart IN 46517
219/293 8633

Triad-Utrad
305 North Bryant Street
Huntington IN 46750

Evaporative Coolers
Dometic
POB 490
Elkhart IN 46515

Redwood Eng.—RECAIR
26690 Wagon Wheel Drive
Pioneer CA 95666
209/295 7556

Trident Rotary
1935 D Friendship Drive
El Cajon CA 92020
619/449 8578

Fluorescent Lights
REC Thin-Lights
530 Constitution Avenue
Camarillo CA 93010
805/987 5021

Theodore Bargman Co.
129 Industrial Avenue
Coldwater MI 49036
1/800 248 2058

Sunalux Corp. (Ballasts)
5955 NW 31st Avenue
Ft. Lauderdale FL 33309
305/973 3230

Generators
Kohler Generators
Kohler WI 53044

Onan Electric Products
1400 72rd Avenue Northeast
Minneapolis MN 55432

Inverters
Heart Interface Corp.
811 First Avenue South
Kent WA 98032
206/859 0640

TRACE Engineering
5917 195th NE
Arlington WA 98223
206/435 8826

Isolators
Sure Power Products, Inc.
10189 Southwest Avery
Tualatin OR 97062
503/692 5360

Refrigeration
Coleman Company
3110 North Mead
Wichita KS 67219
316/832 6532

Dometic
POB 490
Elkhart IN 46515
1/800 544 4881

Marvel Division
PO Box 997
Richmond IN 47374
1/800 428 6644

Norcold
1501 Michigan Street
Sidney OH 45365
513/492 1111

Sibir USA Ltd.
53105 Marin Drive
Elkhart IN 46514
219/264 4777

Sun Frost
PO Box 1101-S
Arcata CA 95521
707/822 9095

Solar Panels/Systems
RV Solar Electric
14415 North 73rd Street
Scottsdale AZ 85260
1/800 999 8520

Surplus Electronics Parts
All Electronics Corporation
905 South Vermont Avenue
PO Box 20406
Los Angeles CA 90006

H&R Corporation
401 East Erie Avenue
Philadelphia PA 19134

Switches & Connectors
Cole Hersee Company
20 Old Colony Avenue
South Boston MA 02127
617/268 2100

Water Tanks & Systems
3-Ts Products (pressure tanks)
15216 Stagg Street
Van Nuys CA 91405
818/782 3405

Marine & Mobile Water (tanks)
5682 Research Drive #C
Huntington Beach CA 92649
714/897 2144

Shurflo (pumps)
12650 Westminster
Santa Ana CA 92706
714/554 7709

Vent Fans & Power Ventilators
Fan-Tastic Vent Corporation
4349 S. Dort Highway/Dept. SES
Burton MI 48529
313/742 0330

Kool-O-Matic
183 Terminal Road
Niles MI 49120
616/683 2600

CAMPING CLUBS

Canadian Family
   Camping Federation
PO Box 397
Rexdale, Ontario,
Canada M9W 1R3

Escapee Club
c/o Kay Peterson
100 Rainbow Drive
Livingston TX 77351
409/327 8873

Family Motor Coach Association
(motorhome owners only)
8291 Clough Pike
Cincinnati OH 45244
513/474 3622
1/800 543 3622

Friendly Roamers
POB 3393, Station S
Northshore CA 92254

Good Sam RV Owners Club
c/o Susan Bray
29901 Agoura Road
Agoura CA 91301
818/991 4980
1/800 423 5061

International Family Recreation
   Association
PO Box 6279
Pensacola FL 32503-0279
904/477 2123

Loners of American, Inc.
Route 2 Box 85E
Ellsinore MO 63967
314/322 5548

Loners on Wheels
808 Lester Street
Poplar Bluff MO 63901
817/626 4538

The National RV Owners Club
PO Drawer 17148
Pensacola FL 32522
904/477 2123

National Campers & Hikers
   Association
c/o Fran Opela
4804 Transit Road
Depew NY 14043
716/668 6242

North American Family Campers
   Association, Inc.
c/o Jeanette Pickles
21 Superior Avenue
Dracut MA 01826
617/459 2836

NATIONAL RV ASSOCIATIONS

Canadian Recreation Vehicle
Association
670 Bloor Street West #200
Toronto, Ontario, Canada MG6 1L2
416/533 4755

Recreation Vehicle
Dealers Association (RVDA)
RV Rental Association (RVRA)
3251 Old Lee
Highway, Suite 500
Fairfax VA 22030
703/591 7130

Recreation Vehicle Industry
Association (RVIA)
1896 Preston White Drive
Reston VA 22090
703/620 6003
PO Box 12455

RVIA Western Office
1748 West Katella, Suite 108
Orange CA 92667
714/531 1688

Handicapped RVers: Contact the RVIA for a listing of manufacturers and
resources.

PV PERIODICALS

Home Power Magazine
PO Box 520
Ashland OR 97520
916/475 3179
$15 per year

PV News
Paul Maycock
PO Box 290
Cassanova VA 22017
$80 per year

Renewable Energy News Digest
861 Central Parkway
Schenectady NY 12309
$60 per year

Solar Electricity Today
Directory of Renewable Energy
Paul Wilkins
2303 Cedros Circle
Santa Fe NM 87505
505/473 1067
$7 per issue

Solar Electric Update
Scottsdale AZ 85260
602/443 8520
Free two-year subscription

BOOKS

Encyclopedia for RVers. Tips on RV living and RV equipment maintenance. Includes listing of RV products and services. $9.95 postpaid from RoVing Press, 100 Rainbow Drive, Livingston TX 77351 (409/327 8873).

Full-time RVing—Complete Guide to Life on the Open Road by Bill and Jan Moeller. $16.95 postpaid from Trailer Life Books, POB 4500, Agoura CA 91301.

Home is Where You Park It by Kay Peterson. $9.45 postpaid from RoVing Press, 100 Rainbow Drive, Livingston TX 77351 (409/327 8873).

Living on 12 Volts with Ample Power by David Smead and Ruth Ishihara. Published by Rides Publishing Company. $25 postpaid from **aatec publications**, PO Box 7119, Ann Arbor MI 48107 (313/995 1470 phone & fax).

The New Solar Electric Home: The Photovoltaics How-To Handbook by Joel Davidson. $21.50 postpaid from **aatec publications**, PO Box 7119, Ann Arbor MI 48107 (313/995 1470 phone & fax).

Practical Photovoltaics by Richard Komp. $19.45 postpaid from **aatec publications**, PO Box 7119, Ann Arbor MI 48107 (313/995 1470 phone & fax).

Survival of the Snow Bird. $8.95 postpaid from RoVing Press, 100 Rainbow Drive, Livingston TX 77351 (409/327 8873).

Index

air conditioning (A/C), 59–60
alternating current (AC), 16
  appliance load guide, 141, 142
  defined, 11
  load planning and switching, 139
alternators, 10, 42–43
ammeter, 15, 108
ampere (amp)
  defined, 11
ampere hour (amp hour), 12
  capacity (battery), 25
appliance consumption worksheet, 86
appliances
  12–volt, & inverters, 55–56
  use, 6–7
  See also individual appliances; sample sys-
    tems

battery, 13, 24
  aging, 30–31
  capacity, 13, 25
  chemical changes, 24
  connections, 121–124
    panel, 19–20
  cycle, 26
    cost per AH, formula, 29
  discharge rate, 25
  drain (table), 132
  equalization charge, 38–39

battery, continued
  life expectancy, 27, 29
  maintenance, 36–38
  overcharging, 42, 46, 75
  placement, 9–10, 31, 32, 33
    See also battery compartments
  precautions, 37
  rating, 27–28
    reserve minutes, 28
  selection, 27–29
  self-discharge, 30–31
  sizing, 89–91, 147–48
    rule of thumb, 90
  specific gravity, 16, 40
  state-of-charge, 16, 25, 39, 41
  sulfation, 30–31
  temperature effects, 29–30
  wiring, 32
battery analyzers, 38–39
battery charging, 14
  conventional, 41–47
  "fast charge," 46
  principles, 41–47
battery compartments, 31–36, 90
  pullout trays, 34
battery types
  automotive, 26, 27
  8–D, 9–10
  golfcart (6–volt), 148